Souls in the Sand

Stories of Setbacks, Surviving,

Stepping and Soaring

Compiled by Lisa Carol Pulliam

for Celia — strong and courageous,
champion for justice, truth seeker,
and beautiful lady — I'm glad to
get to know you. Hope is a beautiful
thing!

Lisa White

Co-authored by

Blenda Aycock

Tara Glasson

Catherine Wade

Carol Thompson

Lisa Pulliam

Trish Holt

Regina Burdett

Kimber Spinks

Lilian Chavira

Sheri Martin

Lisa White

Tracy Tidwell

Courtney Dowdy

Souls in the Sand: Stories of Setbacks, Surviving, Stepping and Soaring

Souls in the Sand: Stories of Setbacks, Surviving, Stepping and Soaring

ISBN: 9781726708630

Dedication

My grandmother Marge was honored when I surprised her by dedicating my first book, *Toes in the Sand*, to her. I treasure an inscription she wrote to me on the dedication page of that book, "Lisa, thank you for remembering me in your journey of life. I'm so proud of you. My love always, Sitti Marge."

This past year has been an incredible adventure, full of ups and downs. Isn't that just life? Chris and I were blessed with our first grandbaby, Emma, and what indescribable joy! Around 6 weeks following Emma's birth, our family gathered to savor a rare and beautiful moment: a five-generation photo with my grandmother Marge, my mom Carol, myself, my daughter Emily, and precious Emma. I will cherish that memory as long as I live.

Several months later, on the morning after my 50th birthday celebration, I received an unexpected phone call from my mom. My grandmother Marge, Sitti (Sit-tee) as we call her, had gone to be with the Lord. I suppose that somewhere deep down I thought she would be with us forever. I had hoped for many more treasured times of sitting at her kitchen table, drinking coffee, laughing at her hilarious stories and learning from her wisdom. After all, I was a grandmother now. Who was more suited to give me advice on this new phase of life than my Sitti? But it was not to be.

As hundreds gathered to celebrate her amazing 96-year life, my sister, brother, cousins and I shared stories, memories, laughter and tears. Oh, how this remarkable woman had impacted our lives and the lives of so many! I had kicked off the new year reading a book given to me by my amazing brother John called *One Word That Will Change your Life*. Through the pages of this book, my One Word for the year slowly emerged: **COURAGE.**

My heart still fresh from the sting of my Sitti's passing, I received another unexpected phone call, this time from Uimpact Publishing Company, asking me to consider compiling a book to encourage and empower women in their journeys. I longed to sit with my grandmother one more time and ask her what I should do. I knew in my soul her answer would be, "Lisa, you can do whatever you set your mind to do... go for it, baby. May God be with you."

So, in memory of my Sitti Marge, a woman who loved deeply, laughed often, overcame many obstacles, and lived a courageous life, I dedicate *Souls in the Sand: Stories of Setbacks, Surviving, Stepping and Soaring* to **you**. If you are a woman who is travelling a challenging road right now, taking shaky steps of faith and longing to soar in your life, please know that the co-authors and I, along with my Sitti Marge say to you, "Go for it, baby. You can do it. Trust in God. It's time to soar."

Table of Contents

Acknowledgments

The authors of *Souls in the Sand: Stories of Setbacks, Surviving, Stepping and Soaring* are deeply grateful for this tremendous opportunity to share a portion of our stories with you. We acknowledge that we have not walked this journey alone. It is with God's grace, provision, companionship, and unfailing love that this project has seen completion and is now being held in your hands and read with your eyes.

We are humbly thankful for supportive family members, spouses, children, parents, and friends who walked with us through the journeys we shared in our chapters, as well as the journey of writing. You showered us with patience and gave us space and freedom to write and create with vulnerability. We are forever grateful for you.

Thank you to the friends, acquaintances, and the many "smart people" in our lives who read our chapters, gave us excellent feedback, and helped us "cross every t and dot every i". How we appreciate your attention to detail and excellence!

Hundreds of photos were submitted for a book cover contest and we congratulate Patti Futch for being the winner! Thank you, Patti, for allowing your special moment on the beach to become a moment of inspiration for so many. The combination of the brilliant, natural colors of God's creation along with the blue lounge chair captivates and beckons the reader to come, sit, and be still for awhile.

Thank you Adorah Tidwell of UImpact Publishing for challenging me to live up to my word for the year: Courage. What a wonderful adventure it has been! A special thanks to Mandy Simmons who has a passion to offer ladies like us the opportunity to share our stories and realize our dreams of becoming authors. Kimberly Pitts, Founder of UImpact, you have impacted my life through coaching, encouragement, and challenging me to dream BIG. How I appreciate you.

And to each co-author, I am so thrilled you said YES to stepping out in great faith and working out your words and your stories with vulnerability and boldness. I know beyond a doubt that the Lord brought us together "for such a time as this." I am in awe of each of you as you walk this road of life possessing two of the most beautiful virtues a woman can possess: courage and humility. May God continue to bless you abundantly as you step into the woman He created you to be. It's time to soar! I love you dearly Soul Sisters,

Lisa

Testimonials

It has been a joy to be a mentor of Lisa's for the past several years. I have watched her grow as an entrepreneur, an author, and a speaker while taking bold steps to do exactly what she inspires many other women to do: STEP into the women they were created to be. Lisa has gathered a courageous group of women around her to contribute to this beautiful new book, *Souls in the Sand*. You will be captivated by these transparent stories and encouraged to soar higher in your faith journey.

Esther Spina

Founder Ambitious Women Conference

www.Estherspina.com

In life we experience hardship, self-doubt, testing, and success. Adulting at times is hard yet also fulfilling. Our experiences lead us to the person we are meant to be. Our souls long to connect with light so we can be a light for others. As you read the stories in this book you will see the light. Be encouraged and know that you too are meant to shine.

Gayle Zientek

Realtor, Entrepreneur and Coach

I met Lisa at First Christian Church in Tyler, Texas but truly became friends after reading her book *Toes In The Sand* and traveling to Israel with Lisa and her husband Chris, who is our pastor, in March of 2018. I admire her openness and her ability to shine even on a dark day! *Souls In The Sand* will touch and inspire everyone who reads it; each author grabs your heart with the turn of every page!

Jeanelle Maland

Member of First Christian Church, Tyler, TX

One of the most beautiful attributes that Lisa has is her uncanny way of making you feel safe and loved at the same time. From the moment I met her, I knew she was someone I could talk to, trust, laugh with (and we always do), and more importantly pray with. It is not every day you meet someone you connect who is real and true. This book is an extension of who she is. Real, loving, honest, inspiring, and thoughtful. She is a woman of God that walks with women in a genuine way while they face real life situations. You will meet other women who will share their personal, raw, and very inspiring stories of their faith journeys with God. This is a must-read book!

Kimberly Pitts

Branding & Marketing Strategist

Founder, UImpact

www.uimpact.net

When I am around Lisa, I cannot help but smile! I love watching her passion exude as she shares stories and life experiences that enable women to leave the struggle behind and step into the women they were created to be. Her books, *Toes in the Sand* and *Souls in the Sand*, translate her passion beautifully and rejuvenate my soul every time I read them as I envision sitting in a chair and turning the heartfelt pages on the sandy shores of a beautiful beach. I highly recommend Lisa's speaking events, women's retreats, and books if you want to experience healing, muster courage, and discover your inner greatness!

Vanessa Buckingham

Web Designer

Co-CEO of MyBizVid

Lisa Pulliam is authentic, heart-centered, wise, and deeply rooted in her faith. She is enthusiastic about helping women find their path spiritually, so they can flourish at home, at work, at church, and in the community. You will be deeply touched getting to know Lisa and each inspiring co-author from the heartfelt stories they share in *Souls in the Sand*.

Alice Hinckley

Entrepreneur / Author / Speaker / Mentor

www.YourLightbulbMoments.com

Introduction

I have always loved sand, the coolness of it in the early mornings, and the heat of it in the afternoons. I eagerly anticipate stepping out onto the beach, flipping off my flip flops and taking that first soft step into this magical sensation.

Doesn't sand feel amazing as it sifts finely through your fingers? Sometimes it can be coarse, made up of tiny sharp rocks and shells. On other beaches, it can be as fine as sugar. After being on the beach all day, I get hungry. My remedy for hunger on the beach is dark chocolate (chocolate is a MUST on the beach!) As soon as this smooth, delicious, melt-in-your-mouth snack hits my taste buds, the sand transforms into a salty, sweet wonder.

Sand. It's just part of the beach experience. If a hurricane washed all the sand away, I would stop going. Sand sets this waterfront experience apart from sitting at the edge of a pool or lake or taking a nice evening bath. It is the source God created to connect the water to the land, almost like the buffer that prepares you for the next experience. Sand is my soul cleanser like a salty spa scrub.

My husband's trademark of a great beach trip is "Mr.Sandman". He and our children spend hours creating a larger-than-life sand man complete with "six pack abs" who lies in the sun with hair and bathing suit made of seaweed. By the end of the day, an innocent passerby might just think he had stumbled upon Mr. America taking a nice afternoon siesta in the sun.

Sand can be delicate, beautiful and so enjoyable. But sand is also gritty… it's salty, rough, drying and can even sting your eyes.

When my granddaughter Emma was just ten months old, we took her to the beach and oh boy was that fun! My daughter Emily covered her fair skin, "untainted by life's harshness", in SPF 75, dressed her in her long-sleeved pink swimsuit and off we went to the beach for Emma's first day of sand and surf! For a little while, Emma was content under the canopy, playing with her toys on a towel. But after a while curiosity took over. She is, after all, my flesh and blood, and she had to experience what I love! Let's just say it is a generational blessing.

"What is that whitish stuff all around me as far as the eye can see???" Emma pondered. And venturing from the safe boundaries of the towel, she crawled a few inches into the big, wide world of sand!

When she first reached for the sand, she grabbed a handful and looked up at us grinning from ear to ear. Then she patted it and pushed it back and forth. Then she grabbed two handfuls and tossed them here and there. Now her hands were covered with sand and she decided to rub the top of her head with it! Grinning, giggling and flashing those five front teeth, she was having too much fun. It was a big morning. But naptime was nearing, and she was getting sleepy. So, what did Emma do next? Before we could say, "Jiminy Cricket" Emma reached up to rub her sleepy eyes. *Oh noooooooooooooo!* It was like a bad movie scene happening in slow motion. We saw it coming but could do nothing to stop it. The tears began to flow as Emma cried, exclaiming in her unspoken way, "Ouch mommy, this hurts!!" We jumped into action, quickly opening water bottles and rinsed her eyes and hands. You can imagine how well this went over! The tears kept coming and the crying got louder. And then, as any good mommy would do, my daughter Emily hopped up with Emma and said, "Well that was fun! Back to the condo for a bath and a nap!"

In the blink…blink…blink, blink… of a sand-filled eye, the fun was over… just like that.

Life is like the wonder of the sand beneath our toes and the ocean beyond it. It can be fun and wonderful and soft and beautiful. We may sit on a towel of familiarity enjoying the sights and sounds around us, but in an instant, everything can change. Dark storm clouds appear out of nowhere and the wind picks up. Without a moment's notice, a gust of wind blows sand in our eyes, leaving us blinded and crying, eyes stinging. Raindrops started to fall; big, hard and forceful. Maybe the storm comes in the way of a dreaded phone call with news that knocks us to our knees, an unexpected turn in a relationship we thought would last forever, a health issue that blindsides us, or a financial situation that seems insurmountable. We wonder when this storm will pass, and if we will ever see the sunny skies and turquoise waters again.

In the pages of this book, you will discover stories of setbacks, struggles, and survival. But, the stories do not stop there. Just as a sunrise brings assurance that a new day is upon us and reminds us that we are being offered another chance, each woman shares her transparent and courageous story with one intention: to inspire, encourage, and reassure you that you are not alone in this journey called life. The darkest night makes way for the most brilliant sunrise. It is in the gritty and most challenging situations, that God touches our souls in the deepest way possible. He can then teach and shape us into the women HE created us to be, women who will soar into the purpose and plan He has for our lives.

How did this group of women of faith come together for *Souls in the Sand*? Great question! It is truly a "God-thing". Several of the authors are beautiful new friends, and I am forever grateful our paths crossed: Carol Thompson, Catherine Wade, Sheri Martin, and Tara Glasson. Several of the gals are "Tocs in the Sand Sisters," having shared life together at my annual Women's Retreat at the beach: Courtney Dowdy, Kimber Spinks, Lilian Chavira, Regina Burdett, and Tracy Tidwell. I treasure their precious friendships. Blenda Aycock and Trish Holt are dear friends whom I met as we all stepped into our entrepreneurial journeys together a few years ago. They have become like sisters to me, and we encourage each other to be bold and courageous in our lives. I have been privileged to know Lisa White the longest, having raised our boys and walked through life together. How I am blessed by her sweet spirit, friendship and encouragement.

As you begin each chapter you will find under the title, one word. This single word speaks volumes. This is the word that inspired each co-author as they shaped their chapter. And friends, God has a word for you.

At the end of each story, each author has included a scripture or favorite quote, and three "Soul Questions" for you to consider. So often we rush through life not stopping to dig deep, notice the little things, practice gratitude, or self-reflect. We invite you to pause at the end of each chapter, consider the questions being asked, and open your soul to an inspirational "ah-ha" moment which might encourage you in your journey. This is our gift to you.

Souls in the Sand

Are you ready?

Close your eyes.

Picture yourself oceanside.

Maybe you're there in the afternoon,

The evening, or during sunrise.

Inhale the salty sea breeze, palm trees swaying.

God's canvas of brilliant colors, a majestic painting.

The soothing sound of the waves rolling onto the shore,

Beckons you to come and seek,

Find rest for your weary soul.

Grab your beverage and some chocolate

We reserved the blue chair for you,

Come and bring your soul to the sand,

For God is here waiting for you.

May God bless you as you step into the woman God created you to be,

Lisa Carol Pulliam

www.stepwithlisa.com

Chapter 1

Tsunami or Wave

"Intentional"

By Blenda Aycock

In March 2005, when I looked into the mirror, I saw a woman a mile wide and an inch deep. I had spread myself thin. I was struggling with being intentional in every realm. I was average in so many things, from organizing project graduation, leading our church youth groups, mission trips, Bible studies, and being active in civic organizations. If you are not intentional, you just have a bunch of good ideas. I was not experiencing abundance, and most definitely not in the overflow of my Christian walk!

As our family was anxiously looking ahead to our son Hunter's high school graduation in just three months, we received some devastating and unexpected news…. Testing had confirmed that Hunter had Type 1 diabetes.

I remember the Doctor telling us that there would be three things that Hunter would never be able to do: go deep-sea scuba diving, pilot a plane, and serve in the military. I felt like the Doctor was trying to comfort me in thinking that my son would never go to war. However, we were in a spiritual battle, and I had not attended boot camp. I had no knowledge or experience in spiritual warfare. My people perish for lack of knowledge (Hosea 4:6).

My mind was racing. I was losing in trying to take my thoughts captive. Would Hunter have a college roommate that would understand his new routine of checking his blood and insulin injections? Would his future wife want this journey? Would he fear becoming a parent? I even mourned my go-to casserole recipes, recognizing they were a carbohydrate nightmare. Waking up every night at 2:00 am monitoring his blood sugar was one of the many adjustments that shifted our daily lives. Life had shifted overnight, and I was overcome with fear! I was too paralyzed to ride the wave and could feel a Tsunami building within my soul. It was like an earthquake beneath a sea of buried pain. I was somewhere between treading water and sinking, with no life preserver in sight. This was the turning point. The trigger of the realization that I needed to let Jesus go deep! It was just a matter of time!

Today, when I walk into a room the first thing on my mind is to make sure everyone feels included. I know that sounds crazy, but the thought of someone being left out hurts me. A kind gesture of a smile or greeting can mean the world to a shy person. People are not invisible and need to be acknowledged. The second thing on my mind is, I wonder if there is dessert in the building! I am serious as a Chocolate cupcake with a cherry on top! I am a foodie at heart. I love to buy, read, and display cookbooks. Plus, I enjoy discovering recipes for my husband to cook! When we travel, we seek FOOD! I will glance at the menu and find myself asking the server EVEN before I order, "What is your dessert specialty?"

I've enjoyed growing up in West Texas, and yes, I have a Texas twang. Can you hear the "southern drawl" come right off the page? My entire family has double names: Billie Faye, Chloe Jane, Mary Lou, Annie Lou, Betty Sue, Wanda Jean, and I am Blenda Gayle! Plus, growing up in the south, you always have dessert and sweet tea! All these double named women love to cook, from flaky cobbler crust to church social casseroles. Hospitality has always been a part of my life. Food is a way to show I care.

When I was nine, I accepted Jesus Christ as my Savior. I had been trained in the word of God and asking him to be my Savior seemed natural. I remember being baptized in the name of the Father, the Son, and the Holy Spirit. I loved God and his son Jesus, but I really knew very little about the POWER of God through the Holy Spirit! No worries; I would mature in my faith! We had a celebration lunch after I was baptized, and my MeMa made cherry cobbler! The word of God does say, *"Taste and see that the Lord is good."* (Psalm 34:8)

My father, Billy Sawyer, worked tirelessly to become a land owner. He purchased a ranch that had a ton of rocks. When I was eleven, painting was a hobby I enjoyed, so it was fitting that I started a rock painting business. With BIG eyes and an even B I G G E R smile, I delivered my first business pitch to my MeMa. I sold her a rock that matched her salt and pepper shakers. And then my PaPa really needed a ladybug painted rock as a paper weight for his desk. I explained to my parents that every bathroom had to have a rock to coordinate with the wallpaper. After all, everyone in the 70's had wallpaper. The only problem was I had more rocks than relatives. Little did I know I was an entrepreneur in the making!

In high school, I was on the debate team. I had dreams of going to Baylor University and becoming a lawyer. God had a different plan. I married young, and soon after started a family. We had two amazing children, Hollie and Hunter.

My days were spent as a full-time volunteer for school, church, and the community. I developed great skills while volunteering, and the value of connecting people was at the top of the list. All these titles and roles became my identity.

My biggest enemy was myself. I had a mindset that I had to be the best at everything. I was in a season where I was wearing too many hats, and not all of them were my style. This is when God warns us, "Do Not Become Weary in Doing Good." (Gal. 6:9). I thrived in the environment of people edifying my strengths and covering my weaknesses.

On August 8th, 2006, 15 months after Hunter was diagnosed, this West Texas lady said, "Ya'll, enough is enough." Can you hear the accent? It is time to experience freedom in Christ! I received ministry for deliverance and inner healing. There had to be a transformation, and it would begin with the renewing of my mind. This was a benefit of my salvation that I did not know existed. When you think differently, you act differently. I was getting tools of freedom. Learning true repentance, forgiving before the sun goes down, and grasping that life and death is in the power of the tongue. Oh my, I started speaking words of LIFE! I stood on the authority of Jesus' name, and strongholds of fear that had taken root when I was a child were uprooted! Having grown up with a brother with diabetes, I began to realize how this illness had been passed down to Hunter and my brother through a generational curse. What is a generational curse? It's anything that keeps repeating itself in the bloodline that is not a blessing; from a poverty mentality, rejection, and addictive traits, to diseases like diabetes.

With JOY I gave Jesus ALL that pain! I felt release, cleansed, made whole, and empowered. I learned that the Holy Spirit was not only within me and for me, but that He would also fall upon me for others. The Holy Spirit began to send me divine appointments to minister. The positive change could not be denied. I remember friends coming up to me asking if I had a face lift, highlighted my hair, different makeup, what was the change? The CHANGE was beauty for ashes! The trade God gives us in (Isaiah 61.)

Ashes represent pain, mourning, suffering; the beauty is the light of Christ radiating in and through us. I was radiating more light! Most of the people I ministered to were mothers. As they received levels of freedom, they noticed some of the same traits of bondage in their children. I began to ask the Lord to help me equip children to be set free. Be careful what you ask for, God may want you to film a video and share it with the world. I followed in obedience. I was empowering others for now and for future generations. You can find this video on YouTube.

When you minister for deliverance, you are pleading the person's case in the very courtroom of God. Lies that hold people bound are exposed, and the TRUTH is revealed. The Truth will set you free, (John 8:32.)

(Isaiah 61) also shares that Jesus comes to set the captives free and release the darkness for the prisoners. It is like being a spiritual lawyer. I really had been given the desires of my heart.

My heart breaks for children who are suffering. Jesus said, *"Let the little children come unto me," (Matthew 19:14.)* I think he had something to tell them. I have learned more and more about how the enemy plants the seeds of lies, in most cases before we are twelve years old. My children were young adults when I received these tools of freedom. If I would've known then what I know now, I would of have parented differently. But I was thankful for becoming fully equipped for my future grandchildren!

Being married to the love of my life is an amazing journey. David is my rudder. Just like a rudder on a ship, he steers and guides me! We've always played it safe when it comes to finances. David was in banking for 23 years, and then helped my dad at a family business for seven years. In the back of his mind he had always wanted to launch into a real estate career. In 2010, it was the season to take the leap. Shifting from getting paid every Friday with benefits, to a career that was totally commissioned based was a new concept. Walking in freedom is so liberating in every realm.

It was my time to use the skills I learned while volunteering, from time management to networking! My confidence was in place to enter the business world; all I needed was to partner with the right company. Direct Sales was a fit for me! I partnered with a company called Ambit Energy. I don't have a college degree, but being an entrepreneur was in my blood. After all, I was the CEO of a successful "rock painting" company at eleven years old!

Connecting people and networking helped my business move quickly. I remember the chorus to one of my favorite childhood songs – the Hokie Pokie! Put your whole self in and your whole self out, PUT YOUR WHOLE SELF IN AND SHAKE IT ALL ABOUT! Were you singing too? My mindset was about surrounding myself with leaders, being teachable, and putting into practice, "if someone else can do it *let them.*" Plus, they all liked the Hokie Pokie! People that put their whole self in are committed, focused, and not afraid of risks. This is important to me, because I did not want to fall into the trap of returning to old mindsets. When you battle fear, you are afraid to take risks.

Both of my children married in December, one year apart! If someone tells you weddings around Christmas are easier, don't believe them! My first granddaughter was born 16 months after our daughter, Hollie, and her husband Matt were married. Her name is Katherine Elizabeth. We call her Kate! I traveled to California the week she was due. She arrived the day I landed. While in the labor room, I laid my hands-on Hollie's belly as we broke generational curses. The day of my first grandchild's birth I was equipped to a new level. I stayed in California for the first 30 days of her life! We spoke powerful declarations over Kate and called forth her identity in Christ. It was perfect having a business that I could operate from my cell phone. My team continued to grow and build; it is all about equipping!

In November of 2013, during our Thanksgiving celebration, my son and his wife Kelsey announced that they were starting the process to foster a child with the intent to adopt. We were overjoyed! My daughter was expecting our second grandchild, and now more grandchildren were on the way. Fostering is a process though. Thankfully, Kelsey and Hunter had huge support from their church. We are grateful for ALL the Body of Christ that walked this adventure with us! We started off by reading books. I suggest reading, "The Connected Child." We attended training, online classes, CPR and wound care certification, house inspections, and more. Not only for parents, but also for anyone you would trust to keep the child at anytime. The people that come along beside you to this level are called wrap around families. They wrap you with love, prayers, and physical support. If you need to go to the grocery store, only your wrap around family can keep the child.

March 2014 came in roaring like a lion! My birthday was on the 6th. I only had a few days to hit my business goal of promoting to Executive Consultant before my 50th birthday! Precious friends held a baby shower for Kelsey on the first Saturday in March. All the requirements for fostering had been met. We were told it would take two weeks to process all the info in the system. Our daughter had come home for the shower. As we were driving Hollie to the airport to head back to California, I was notified that I had just promoted to Executive Consultant! This is a huge accomplishment and can only be done with massive teamwork. With a few days to spare, I had hit my Goal! The more you make, the more you can give. Plus, I had all these grandkids coming!

I was working on building my new Executive Franchise when my phone rang. It was Hunter, and he asked if I was sitting down. My heart raced as I thought how could this be the call? There was no way the state of Texas got all the paper work processed so fast. Well, he told me there were newborn twin girls that were being placed in 24 hours! The state had contacted four other families, and they were not able to take the twins at this time. Miraculously, they would expedite their paperwork if they would agree to take the girls! Hunter and Kelsey said yes! They were on their way to the hospital to spend the night and bring them home the next day! As I hung up the phone, my mind pressed replay of all the things that Hunter had been robbed of with the pain of diabetes. And God in his extravagance had given Hunter more than he could dream or imagine. A precious bride that also had a heart to foster a child. And in the Father's abundance, the blessing was DOUBLED!

My mom and I loaded up the car and headed out of town to meet the girls. Kelsey and a friend were rocking them in the NICU when we arrived. I will never forget the first time I saw them. They were so very innocent and helpless. I remembered that the Holy Spirit would fall upon me to help others. I felt that tingling sensation in me. And I knew it was TIME to share it with these perfect, yet teacup-sized, babies! I laid my hands on the girls' tiny, little chests and decreed over them, "You are loved, you are safe, and you are accepted." They slept in my arms in perfect peace as their spirit bore witness to the presence of God. We broke the power of rejection and addiction in the mighty name of Jesus! ALL authority in heaven and on earth has been given to us in the name of Jesus. (Matthew 28:18). We spoke life, and life abundantly over them, and decreed that no weapon formed against them shall prosper! They were dismissed from the hospital the next day, on my 50th birthday! We celebrated with a giant decorated chocolate chip cookie, not knowing whether these precious girls might be a part of our lives for a paragraph, a page, a chapter, or a lifetime. Goodness, in less than a week I had promoted to Executive Consultant, had two new grandchildren, and turned 50! Things were moving so fast! Was this another Tsunami, or a wave? Only time would tell!

Many well-meaning people began to speak to us about our tiny twins, "You really need to guard you heart" and "Don't get too attached." We made a family decision that these baby girls deserved 100% of our love. We knew if they had to leave and go back to the birth parents, it would be heartbreaking, but we reminded each other that Jesus was the binder of the brokenhearted!

I knew very little about the foster process. I had no clue that we had to keep a journal of everything that happened every day. We recorded everything times TWO! Every diaper change; the first day we went through 32 diapers! In between changing babies and feedings, we scribbled how many ounces they drank and if they spit up. They even wanted to know the preferences of these precious babies. Did they like to be swaddled? What kind of bottle and pacifier did they use? Did they take naps; what time, how long? It was bittersweet, because we knew we were recording all this information in case they were removed from our care. The next person needed to know the schedule. There is security in familiar!

The girls loved music. We played praise and worship music, read to them, and prayed in POWER over them! The love and support of family, friends, neighbors, and the Body of Christ was a blessing! It really does take a village. I know foster care or adoption is not for everyone, but everyone can contribute. Pure and lasting religion in the sight of God our Father means that we must care for orphans and widows in their troubles and refuse to let the world corrupt us. (James 1:27). People helped with meals, gift cards for take-out meals, mowing the grass, and diapers even showed up on the front porch. We had five wrap around families that could help with the girls, and we needed all of them! Did I mention all the continual home visits by CPS and the Adoption Agency, New Horizons? People stopped by to check on the girls, inspect the home, determine their progress, support us, connect us to physical, occupational, and speech therapy if needed. They reminded us of all the doctor and dentist appointments, as well as helped us stay in touch with the lawyers. Plus, they helped us stay on task with parental visits and all the hearings. The birth parents, by choice, only visited the girls one time. Hunter and Kelsey met them and assured them the girls were safe and loved. We treasured every day and began to ride the wave!

I stayed for three weeks straight and visited them weekly for months. I remember showing my son how to bathe a tiny little soul that weighed less than five pounds. My heart was bursting with joy. Watching your children parent is so fun! I was intentional in being fully focused on whatever or whoever was in front of me. While they napped, I did laundry, read cookbooks with more sugar free recipes, and worked on my business. You really can build a full-time income PART-TIME! I even qualified for a FIVE STAR TRIP with the leaders of my company, a desperately needed luxury getaway for me and David several months after the twins arrived. This trip not only was a reward, but the trip of my dreams. A 5-star resort hotel, including everything from a beach front view to a private butler. Thank you, Ambit Energy! This company is such a blessing to me.

During the craziness of my life back home, I had felt like a maid at times! But, during this beautiful all-expense vacation, David and I had our own butler who brought us dessert, coffee and anything we needed. This was a pure treat. Watching a butler pack my luggage while I read a book and ate a buffet of mouthwatering desserts is just what I needed! God is so fun!

Six weeks after the 5-Star trip, I headed back to California to prepare for the birth of my daughter's 2nd baby. Avery Anneliese was born in May. It was a special time loving, blessing and praying over her. Wow, 3 granddaughters born in less than 4 months. I stayed in California for almost a month. Hollie and Matt had a 2-year-old and a newborn. At this point, I was like a baby whisperer. With Jesus' help, I balanced household chores, growing a business, and ministry opportunities. While the girls napped, I would go to, drum roll please......... a local bakery! I enjoyed just a taste of cookie or muffin, made calls for my business, and snoozed for 10 minutes in my car to allow my body to process all the sugar! And how about my husband? He was a saint! This was one wild WAVE of life changing events we experienced!!!!

We are not created to do everything. When your mind tells you that you need to be super woman, you are headed for burnout! That is why in family, business, ministry and life you need to delegate and multiply, but most of all, take the time TO BE STILL and know that He is God! I also share with my children that one of the best examples I can model for them is a Godly marriage. You must take time for your spouse! There were so many things happening at the same time during that time in our lives. We learned to say, "This is what I can do, but I can't do everything." The enemy tempts us to feel isolated and do everything on our own. We are created to be a part of the Body of Christ. We need to communicate and work functioning body. This was my same guideline for business partners as well. I had to come to a place of equipping, not enabling. I am still learning this lesson!

In the middle of an exploding business and grandkids popping up everywhere, God opened a door for me to speak at Christ for the Nations in October of the same year! This organization's focus is to impact humanity with the Gospel of Jesus Christ. Christ for the Nations is an educational institute. They host several conferences each year. I spoke at the Voice of Healing Conference. My video that was made to equip children appeared to be getting the attention of many! I also qualified for a 2nd Five-Star trip with my company. While I enjoyed the sand and sea air, I made final preparations for the sessions I would lead. My topic was setting the captives free. Breathless, refreshed and rejuvenated, we left the beautiful sandy beaches in Mexico. I jumped into a taxi the moment we landed in Dallas to zip on over to speak at Christ For the Nations the next day. Over 90 nations were represented! I witnessed (Psalm 46:10) ....in the faces of all these people from all over the earth. "I will be exalted to the NATIONS!"

Did you know that November is National Adoption Month? We had so hoped the adoption could be final by then, and we were already planning a Gotcha Day. A Gotcha Day is a phrase that denotes the anniversary of the day on which a new member joins a family in the adoption process. Adoption pictures are taken with each child, with a sign stating how many days they were in the adoption process. Today, just as back then, there are thousands of children in our nation and world that need families.

Our lawyer, Jody Fauley, was outstanding. He had a huge passion for adoption. He kept us so informed, as this was a process that we had no experience in. He wanted us to be realistic and felt it would be close to a year before things would be final!

November arrived, and both the birth mother and father needed to agree to terminate their rights. At the very last hearing, the birth father showed up and wanted the girls. He was given 5 days to really weigh this decision out with an educated council. Holding our breath, and praying fervently, we were thrilled to receive the news that the father had decided to terminate his rights! These precious gifts from God were ours forever! We had avoided the Tsunami, and the adoption wave had carried us safely to shore!

Abbey Ruth and Addie Faye, at the sound of the gavel, were Aycock's! Their adoption sign reads 259 Days! Did you catch the double names?! They inherited middle names from two extraordinary women. Ruth is my husband's mother's middle name, and Faye is my mother's middle name.

Adoption is powerful in the natural, but a miracle in the Spirit! You have not received the spirit of bondage, again to fear, but you have received the Spirit of adoption, whereby we cry Abba Father (Romans 8:15).

Life in the present! God has created me to be a woman that is bold, strong, and courageous. He has also created me to be calm, nurturing, and to remind myself that it is ok to BE STILL, and perfectly fine to have a bite of a cookie every day at 4:00 PM! The Lord continues to teach me the progress that can happen when I am *Intentional.* God was so intentional in sending His one and only son. I find peace in knowing that I too am adopted into the Kingdom of God, and I find joy in sharing salvation with everyone I meet. You can find me teaching tools of freedom at events or on YouTube. I continue to embrace being an entrepreneur. I cherish every season of life with my family. God gives me many platforms to share His love through our story! I serve on boards that impact children, from autism to foster care. God's faithfulness keeps me steady! He is the God of Abraham, Isaac, Jacob, and Blenda Gayle!

Our NEW WAVE includes grandsons; Hollie and Matt had our first prince, Carter Lewis, in 2017!

And Hunter and Kelsey are expecting their first son in November of 2018!

Be STILL and KNOW that I am God. I will be exalted among the nations, and I will be exalted in the earth. (Psalm 46:10)

Soul Questions

- Have you ever felt a tsunami crashing down on your life? If so, write about it and share how you walked through that season.

- I learned in a very full season of life that I had to be intentional with family, ministry, business, and especially taking time to be still. In what area of your life do you want to be more Intentional?

- Read (Isaiah 61:3) God loves to exchange pain for freedom. I traded ashes for beauty! Is there anything that you would like to trade?

I love God, I love learning, and I LOVE sharing the things that I have learned! Stay in touch by going to BlendaAycock.com or email me at BlendaAycock@gmail.com

Blenda Aycock

Blenda Aycock loves God, loves learning, and loves sharing what she has learned. She enjoys building relationships with people of all ages, backgrounds, and cultures. Her favorite question is "How can I best support you"? The more you know how to support others the more you can connect them to a solution!

Blenda's professional career includes the direct sales arena. Reaching the level of Executive Consultant allows her the benefit of Residual income. Time freedom gives her the joy for family and ministry. She is an ordained minister and loves to worship. Being on the ministry team at her church home, Freedom Fellowship, in San Angelo, Tx. is one of her greatest joys. She has taught the Freedom Foundation Class to hundreds and is passionate about giving people the tools to walk in freedom. You can find her video on the church website under Children's Ministry. WWW.FreedomFellowship.US

She is a member of Texas Business Women and has won speaking events on the State level with this organization. Blenda is active in her West Texas community and serves on several boards including the Arc of San Angelo that supports people of all ages in the autism spectrum and more. She also serves on the Greater Concho Valley Community Partners for Children. This board supports the Rainbow Room, that supplies items that are needed for the first 48 hours that a child is in foster care.

When Blenda learns something new she is passionate about sharing. Her speaking platform ranges from zoom meetings, to Bible Studies, business trainings, and Christ For the Nations.

Her husband, David, of 36 years is the love of her life! They are blessed with 2 children, 5 grandchildren and more on the way!

At the end of the day Blenda can be found on her family farm reading cookbooks and finding recipes for her husband to prepare. She is a professional tester of all things SWEET!

Chapter 2

Riding the Emotional Waves

"Worthy"

By: Tara Glasson

We all have a story. I am honored to share a small piece of mine. The enemy kept me from writing it for many years. The enemy was FEAR. I had to let FAITH into my life for this story to happen. My sweet Mom always told me that Faith and Fear cannot live in the same home. I think God was telling me to be patient and trust my journey. I certainly would not have been able to share my story, if I would have done things my way. My story starts when I was ten years old.

In 1975, my family returned to the United States, after my father had completed a two-year overseas assignment on the island of Crete, Greece. He was the deputy base commander, and we lived near the Mediterranean while there. He finished his military career in San Antonio, Texas, which I call my hometown. I have always loved to walk on the beach, but I have never liked swimming or riding the waves in the ocean. As an innocent 10-year-old, I could have never imagined anything more beautiful that staring at the blue waters being lost in my innocence. I was happy and carefree and had a wonderful childhood until my teenage years. Fast forward to the age of 26; I made Corpus Christi, Texas my home, and I live 20 minutes from the ocean. But, I enjoy walking and staring at the ocean from such a different view now than when I was ten years old. I have always feared high waves that could send me further from the shore and far into unknown waters. I compare those waves to the emotional waves we all face daily.

Throughout my life, I have had to fight through many Emotional Waves, heading out to the ocean farther than I would have liked. Emotional waves of insecurity, betrayal, marital issues, addiction, loss of identity, depression, anxiety, challenges of motherhood, and more. There are a few I would like to share.

Emotional Wave of Acceptance

My Dad was a great man, but very controlling during my upbringing. During my teenage years, I never thought I could please him or my Mom. My older brother was the one that received all the honors and grades, and I just never felt like I could live up to the expectations on me. Of course, parents love their children equally and unconditionally, right? Yes, I realize that, now that I myself am a mom. Back then, I became rebellious and wanted acceptance from peers and anyone who would accept me for me. I made some poor choices during my high school, college, and young adult years. I poured so much guilt and shame on myself for years due to those choices. I now realize the past is the past, and one must move forward. But, those years held me back for a long time, keeping me stuck and unable to let go, move forward and trust again. During those insecure years, I came across strong, but was really broken on the inside. I became even more insecure and wanted to be accepted for all the wrong reasons. This led to depression, anxiety and toxic relationships especially with men. God was not the focal point of my life, even though I had attended a Christian University. Everywhere I went I seemed to put on more layers of my mask and hide my real emotions. Through lots of prayer and growth, I eventually learned that I could not please everyone. It has taken many years to reverse that negative self-talk in my head and know I am worthy. Also, I've found my identity through my relationship with God. HE loves me and did not make junk.

Sadly, my father passed away at age 60, of a sudden heart attack. He left this earth just six months after he walked me down the aisle towards an awesome man! I tried so hard to please my father for so many years, and then God took him before he could see how happy I was as a wife and mom. Once my Dad passed, I was able to reflect and see how he truly did love me. He had his way of showing that love through strict rules and control. As I grew in self-awareness and healing through my journey, I was able to say, "Yes, I am worthy!"

Emotional Wave of Depression

Reflecting to my teenage years, I have always battled depression. Though I was not sure what I was dealing with until I became an adult. It has affected how I have dealt with life's daily issues. I can best describe it as being a "prisoner" in my own body. Many Christians might be quick to say, "Just pray about what is bothering you. Stay away from medication." Well, sometimes a pill takes the edge off and keeps me near the shore, rather than being dragged into the depths of the dark ocean.

One of the moments when I struggled the most was in January of 2008. I was the Director at our church's Mother's Day Out program. I was getting frustrated about the "pettiness" that came with this position and bewildered by how much backstabbing could be happening in a place of worship. Unfortunately, this happens everywhere. I continued to keep layering on my mask, but on January 20th, 2008, I finally took off my mask. I was exhausted from the mixture of emotions, panic and self-doubt. I was sitting in Bible Class, and I went into an anxiety attack. I could not quit crying. Immediately, I went to my office, pulled out a notepad and began writing. God had HIS hand in this moment. At our church, we sing an "invitational" song after the lesson, and anyone that wants to request prayers goes forward in front of the congregation. On that day, I did not hesitate. I wanted my husband's uncle, Buck Griffith, to read my note to the church and pray over me. He had been the pulpit minister for years, and he continues to be a mentor and wonderful example.

"I pray that this prayer request will be lifted up in prayer. As humans, we have the temptation to make assumptions and talk amongst each other. This prayer request is lifted to the Lord to help me battle a continuous cycle of depression. One might ask why Tara would even begin to suffer from this illness? Tara has a wonderful and supportive husband, two precious children and numerous blessings each day of her life. She is not battling CANCER and doesn't have a loved one at war. Depression is an illness. It can become overwhelming and exhausting to put on the perfect mask each day. That is why I am asking for prayers and encouragement to peel the mask away and lean on the only One who can cure me. Our Lord Jesus Christ. I want to survive this daily battle to help other women who silently struggle with depression. Pray for our family as I continue to be the best Christian wife and mother the Lord and myself want me to be. I thank you for the sincerity of all prayers lifted up for me."

I felt so free! For so long, depression has been a topic that most do not want to admit they struggle with. However, the more I have visited with women over the years, the more they have shared about how they have dealt with their depression. I lifted them up in prayer and was no longer ashamed to be carrying this burden. What is important is to recognize the symptoms and get the appropriate help. It is NEVER too late. Do not be ashamed to reach out, take off the mask of feeling the need to be STRONG and take the necessary steps to find someone you can trust with how you are feeling. We are WORTHY!

Emotional Wave of Identity-Who am I?

I have been blessed to be able to stay home with my children. It has not always been easy. Days were long due to the children being bad asthmatics. I missed my career, but me and my husband made the financial sacrifices for me to stay home. After adjusting to staying home 24/7, I threw myself into volunteering for my children's schools as they began pre-school and grade school. I also taught a college class online for a couple of years, but I was still tied to home while the children were at school. I continued to struggle with finding myself. Finally, I decided to go back to school for another certification. I had never pursued my LPC in Counseling, due to FEAR, but I wanted to find a way to move forward and help other women, along with myself. I had never taken time to focus on myself. I wanted to make sure I was the perfect daughter, daughter-in-law, wife, mother and on and on the list went...which had led me further into the dreaded deep.

Finally, I found a wonderful coaching school called PCCI (Professional Christian Coaching Institute) and began my journey of life coaching. It was an online school, so I took classes and coached online. I met the most incredible people and stayed in touch with my coaching peers. I wanted to do something for me, for *Tara,* and it felt great. My advice for everyone is to not lose your identity! Seek God for your path and take time for YOU!

I had to make time for myself and not feel guilty about it. So, I developed a website and prepared myself for women to email me wanting to be coached. Well, that didn't happen, and I hit a wall! At that time, God was telling me that I still needed to grow. I had a story to share, but it was not ready yet. Remember the prayer request back in 2008?

Emotional Tidal Wave of Illness

God's timing is so amazing, and I cannot begin to tell you all the ways HE worked in my life during 2016 and how much I have grown in FAITH. After a storm, there is always a rainbow and a purpose. As you have noticed, I am not one to sit still. God was about to calm the waves and share with me something so profound; *"Be still and Know that I am God." (Psalm 46:10)*

In the Fall of 2015, I went back to our Mother's Day Out program at our church, this time as a classroom teacher for Pre-K. I loved my precious co-teacher, Jodie. My sister-in-law, Marcia, was teaching in another classroom next to me. It was so much fun, and I loved being around Christian women two days a week. Honestly, I have always preferred older children, but this was just what I needed. It was fun hearing little giggles, wiping tears, singing songs, tying shoes and loved the many hugs! God's timing was perfect!

Like 9/11, there are certain dates one never forgets. On March 4th, 2016, I received a phone call that no one ever wants to receive. I was told I had breast cancer. How can something so small wreak such havoc on one's body? I was so upset, and I still go through the occasional emotions of confusion and anger to this day. I remember calling my husband who rushed home immediately. Next, I called my brother. My brother and his family live in Boerne, Texas, about 30 minutes from San Antonio. I hoped he could go tell our Mom in person. He had just walked through the door of his house. He was blown away with his own storm on the same day. Then, he proceeded to tell me that his highly ranked position had been eliminated after 11 years of work. What? The watershed of emotions began! I felt shock, numbness and so many other emotions that I wanted to hide from my children. I had to keep it together until I could process these events in my mind. God began working overtime for our families during the following months, and we were brought closer together through the storm.

There were so many decisions to be made, and the waiting was driving me crazy! As humans, we want answers immediately! I finally chose to stay local, have a lumpectomy and get six weeks of radiation. Thankfully, I was in Stage 1 when my cancer was discovered, and I am now in remission. Many friendships were built and renewed during this time in my life. I had a strong support system, and my tribe grew! I will always be forever grateful to my friend, Pam, who encouraged me DAILY with early morning texts and organizing meals. Nelda, a dear friend who sent me beautiful emojis and prayers each night before I went to sleep. Another person in my support system was a survivor and an inspiration. She and her daughter made me a beautiful breast cancer blanket which will be forever cherished. Another was going through the same journey, and we continue to remain close, having been "cancer sisters."

My husband never left my side for appointments and surgeries. My co-workers would pray for me while I could not work. Another precious friend, Missie, played a huge role. She gave me a clinging cross to hold, and I took it with me to my radiation appointments and would spend that time in prayer. I went early so I could get home, wake up the kids and get them to school. Normalcy was important for me during this time. Also, I felt at peace. I attribute it to all the prayer warriors that were praying for me and my family during this time; FERVENTLY praying from all over the country. I was humbled to be added to many prayer lists and prayer groups. Mike, a pathologist and Missie's husband, called me with the results. The cancer was gone and was so small it had come out during the biopsies. PRAISE GOD!!! Having a positive attitude was half the battle! Although, during my course of treatments, I noticed something peculiar with my daughter's neck. It was almost time for her checkup, so I decided to wait and not worry too much about the gradual swelling in her neck.

I was about to turn 50 that July, and I was nearing the end of radiation treatments. I wanted to select a special day to have my last treatment, a day I would always remember. I chose my son's birthday, June 15, 2016. He was at church camp, but I wanted to remember this victory every year on his birthday. Marcia and her friend, Annie, put on quite a celebration for me at our home. My precious Morgan has a beautiful voice and sang to me in front of many of my awesome prayer warriors and fellow cancer sisters. June 15th was a wonderful day to remember forever! Shortly after our celebration, a phone call came from our son, asking if his father would baptize him at Camp Bandina on Friday evening. I went to bed crying tears of joy that night! There were so many emotional waves during this part of my journey.

As we savored God's blessings of healing and new life in our family, I reflected on the journey I had traveled. Life was certainly a wild ride, sometimes being lifted high on the waves of provision and answered prayer, other times crashing down and being pulled under the water again.

My daughter, Morgan, was diagnosed with Hashimoto's disease when she was 14. She had been seeing a pediatric endocrinologist every six months to check her thyroid levels. At her check-up the doctor requested a biopsy. So, that Friday morning, before we left for Camp Bandina to witness Grant's baptism, Morgan had a biopsy on her thyroid gland. The day of Grant's baptism proceeded to be a glorious day. The following morning, Hannah, who is my niece, Morgan and I flew to Dallas to see Selena Gomez in concert. My emotions were all over the place at that time...many tears of joy and thankfulness and being ready to move forward with some normalcy. The girls had so much fun at the concert, and I enjoyed relaxing.

Monday morning the phone rang, and it was Mike, our dear friend and pathologist. He said, "Tara, the Glasson's cannot seem to catch a break." He told me that Morgan had papillary thyroid cancer. What?! I fell to my knees and could not breathe. I had just finished treatments five days ago, and now my precious daughter had a battle to fight. I just remember shouting and asking God, "WHY?" I called my husband, who rushed home immediately, and we cried together.

God went to work immediately, and that week was filled with confusion, tears, and trying to figure out which direction to go, once more. I will be forever grateful that my friend, Shelley, made a call to an ENT and surgery was scheduled. Morgan was entering her senior year of high school in late July, and we needed a plan of action. Unfortunately, in the middle of all this, that following Friday, Morgan went to run an errand and got in a car accident. She failed to yield at a busy intersection, and a car hit her on the passenger side. Her car was totaled and tipped over. By God's amazing grace, angels came and pulled her out of the car and carried her to the curb until we got there. She had not one scratch, and her phone was still intact to call me. Thankfully, the other woman did not have a scratch on her either. However, Morgan was served with lawsuit papers. These circumstances found me both thankful and beginning to question my Faith at the same time.

I had hit a breaking point and felt like I could not come up for air. I was riding all the waves and was far from shore, DEEP into the ocean waters. Immediately, prayer warriors and friends took over and delivered meals, gift cards and continuous prayers. My friend, Iris and her daughter, Bella, along with others designed a bracelet in thyroid colors. The bracelet said, "Team Morgan, No One Fights Alone."

The bracelets were such an encouragement to Morgan when she saw the bracelet on someone's wrist. Her surgery was successful, and she did have to have a total thyroidectomy. She was released

on July 4th, one of her favorite holidays. She considers that victory as her own Independence Day. She was tired for so long. We took her to MD Anderson for a second opinion for treatments and she did not need to have any further treatments. She made a YouTube video describing our journey. *

We made a pact that Cancer would not define us. Also, the lawsuit was settled, though it hung over us for a long time. During all the craziness, some of my dear high school friends traveled to Port Aransas to ring in our 50th birthdays. They surprised me one night by wearing pink t-shirts that said, "Tara's Tribe: No one fights alone." Their support really helped me handle all that was going on. Also, when I turned 50 on July 24th, my friends from my son's soccer years kidnapped me and took me to South Padre for the weekend! Thank you to Velma, Lena, and Kitay for helping me "belly" laugh again! I'll be forever grateful for ALL my special friendships.

That Fall, our son kept us happily distracted with all his sports activities, and we finally got back to normal. So much had also happened in our extended families that year. It was time to breathe and find my way back to shore.

*Morgan's YouTube link: MY STORY: 2 YEARS LATER youtu.be (Morgan G)

Moving Forward

I slipped back into those dark waters of depression and anxiety, but God brought me back to shore and my faith began to strengthen again over fear. I have become very close to friends in a Friday morning prayer group where we specifically pray for our children. Also, a life changing season came again for me when I gathered with some church friends and studied the book, <u>Fervent</u>, by Priscilla Shirer. I had no idea how much the ENEMY was playing a significant role in my life for so long, and in many different situations.

Motherhood has had its challenges. I just laugh now at how I felt I had to be the perfect Mom and have it all together. Moms need to look frazzled! That means YOU are doing a great job. There is no perfect way to "parent." Do not compare and remember, "YOU ARE WORTHY!"

Marriage has had its trials. We were at a crossroads when the children were younger, as well as in recent years, due to betrayal and addiction. It requires lots of compromise, forgiveness and unconditional love. As years go on, some marriages go on auto-pilot, and parents get so wrapped up in their children. One day, the children will be young adults, grown and starting their own family. Take time for you and your spouse. I still wonder how God brought me and Craig together. I was the crazy "party" girl, and he has never been inebriated! I am his crazy. I made a mistake of putting him on a "pedestal." No one is perfect, but I had never met a man who was so kind to me. We balance each other, and only God could have made this work!

Lastly, I must not leave this person out of my story. It is my precious Mom, who has loved me unconditionally. She is getting older, and I want her to stay on this journey with me! I will be forever grateful for her being such a strong, compassionate and caring Mom during my victories and defeats. Awesome and positive…always in my corner!

"Sometimes the most difficult part of any journey is believing that you're worthy of the destination. The one where you see that goal, that dream or what it is that you have always longed for. You are brave enough to face the challenges, and strong enough to see it through the end. Never be afraid to take that first step. With each new step, bringing you closer to it. Believe it! You can do it."

Brigitte Nicole

(Inspirational Quotes Club)

Soul Questions

- Have you ever felt you are not worthy? Believe in YOU! What steps can you take to make you feel worthy?

- God does not make JUNK. YOU were made in HIS image. How can you let go of all the negative self-talk and move forward to what God has intended you to become?

- Reflecting on the choices you have made in your life, have you made them for yourself or to please others? How can you transform future choices into glorifying God?

I do not know the rest of my story, but I know that God has already written it for me and for you. I would describe myself as broken through parts of my journey without much direction. Confidently, God has paved the way for me through the many challenges of motherhood, marriage and friendships, to finally be True2ME! Don't sink, but be strong, courageous and SWIM! Be True2U and write me at tara@true2ucoaching.com and let me know how you relate to this chapter. To God be the Glory!

Hugs, Tara

Tara Glasson

 Tara Glasson is a graduate with a degree in Education from Abilene Christian University and received a Masters in Counseling from Texas A&M University in Corpus Christi, Texas. Tara was a classroom teacher for ten years and has been a very busy stay at home Mom volunteering for various organizations and her children's schools.

Tara has completed her training with PCCI (Professional Christian Coaching Institute) to receive certification and is a life coach.

While training is instrumental with Tara's career, she believes her own experiences of walking through challenges of motherhood, marriage, depression, self-esteem issues, fear, anxiety and cancer will offer her a unique perspective, empathy, and passion for helping one through her journey. Tara embraces the challenge of helping other women find their inner peace and become true to themselves.

Tara resides in Corpus Christi, Texas with her husband and two children.

Tara's coaching website is www.true2ucoaching.com

Chapter 3

Hidden in the Sand

"Loved"

By Catherine Wade

Have you ever walked along the seashore looking for the perfect shell? You know, the one that is just the right shape, size and color. The one that no one else has. The one that is the most difficult to find because it is usually hidden beneath layers of sand. The one that will be the talk of the beach trip for years to come. You know…the PERFECT one!

So many times, over the years I have done just that. I have spent hours walking along the seashore looking for the "perfect" shell. I didn't do it, however, for the bragging rights it would give me. The truth is, I did it because deep within the recesses of my heart, there was a desperate need to be perfect myself. I believed that perfection would command the approval, acceptance, recognition and even the love that my heart yearned for since the day my father abandoned me as a young child.

For the longest time I had the twisted idea that if I would have been just good enough, or less trouble…if I would have been perfect…he would have never left. He would have never deserted me! He would have never left me with a spirit of rejection and a skewed idea of what love was and how it behaved.

As the years passed, my need for perfection, acceptance, approval and most of all love, only intensified. Because of my twisted and skewed reality of what that was supposed to look like, it became a destructive force in every aspect of my life. It affected how I approached school, how I took care of my home, my friendships, my marriage and how I raised my children. Finally, it even affected how I approached my relationship with God. My entire being was a stressed out, miserable, empty mess. I was hopeless, but at the same time, I was driven to achieve perfection.

While some may say trying your best is not a bad thing, let me just say that I would agree. However, to be driven to the point of self-abasement, then it's a horrific, destructive force to be reckoned with in all areas of one's life. I was like an EF5 tornado! I left destruction everywhere I went, some of which was not repairable. None of that, though, mattered to me since I was driven by my internal, desperate need to find acceptance – to find love. I was self-absorbed. I was determined beyond reason that no one would ever have a motive to reject, leave or never love me again. I was on a mission to be perfect. Perfection, after all, equated to my being accepted…wanted…loved!

In school, I would spend hours on end studying to achieve that all-encompassing grade of an "A" on my work or on a test. I had to be the best! I had to be first to finish. I had to be the one that others would turn to for information. I always had to be on top of my game and nothing nor anyone, not even my family, could get in the way of that. I thrived on the attention and accolades that my driving force afforded me daily. I thrived on the recognition and the twisted feeling of love and acceptance it gave me. I was not about to lose it, too, just as I had lost my father's! While I graduated Suma Cum Laude and one of eleven valedictorians of a graduating class of approximately nine hundred and fifty students, the congratulations I received wasn't enough. I still walked away with my gold collegiate braids hanging around my neck and an emptiness and longing within my soul. Oh yes, there was a smile on my face but not for the reasons you would think. The forced smile was a façade I had learned over the years. I had to keep up the appearance that everything about me and my life was flawless, while on the inside there was a little girl crying and screaming to the top of her lungs, WHY? Why wasn't I happy? Why did I still feel so lost? Why was there still such an undeniable sense of loneliness and emptiness within? After all, I had achieved my goal, hadn't I? My anguish and despair of ever finding love only deepened as I walked away from the coliseum that day.

To my chagrin, however, school was not the only place my irrational behavior played a role. The way I maintained my home is, yet another story of ultimate misery perpetuated from a need to be flawless. Misery beyond measure was dispensed on all who lived and/or entered my front door. I was a clean freak! Nothing could be out of place. Even the spacing between the pictures on the walls had to be perfect, and the streaks in the rug from vacuuming had to be aligned just right. From the minute someone's foot hit the floor in the morning, beds had to be made in such a way that military personnel could learn a thing or two on the proper way to make a bed. Clothes and shoes belonged in only one place - the dresser drawer and/or the closet. Every article of clothing and pairs of shoes had to be color coded and organized in a specific way. At no time could you just stuff them in the dresser drawer or throw them in the closet or even lay them on a chair to be put away later. That was considered taboo! The kitchen was kept cleaned even while a meal was being prepared. The sight of dishes in the kitchen sink would turn my stomach to the point of severe nausea, as it would remind me of the filth I grew up in as a child after my father left. But that is another story for a later time! No one was ever allowed to place anything, such as a dirty cup, spoon, bowl or plate in the sink. Even leaving a dirty dish on the counter was forbidden. Everything had to be placed in the dishwasher without hesitation for the appearance of excellence to be maintained. Heaven forbid, if I was in the middle of washing and folding clothes and someone would show up without notice…I would go into crisis mode! The clothes would immediately be thrown back into the dryer and out of sight. I ask you, who does that? Of course, I did because everything had to appear flawless. I would even go as far as to empty an ash tray every time a flick of ashes found their way in it from our friends who smoked. Pointless to say, my friends stopped coming over or calling me to do things with them. While they never explained to me what I had done wrong and why they no longer wanted to be my friend, I knew! Deep in my heart, I knew! I knew I was difficult to be around and to keep happy. I was never satisfied. I was always negative about every aspect of my life, my home and my family. Since I was so critical of my own imperfect world, I made others feel less than adequate in theirs. I was consumed, and it was beyond anyone's ability to make or keep me happy or satisfied on a consistent basis. Sheer misery for all, even myself, just because of a deep seeded need within me to be wanted and loved. Regardless of how hard I tried to create a perfect environment that would satisfy my longings, at the end of the day, I continued to feel abandoned and totally worthless.

The sense of worthlessness followed me everywhere. It appears there was nothing I could do to escape it! It even reared its ugly, destructive head in my relationship with my husband and our three sons and daughter. There are no words to describe the amount of anguish my actions toward them brought to my heart then and even today. After all, the one thing I had hungered for my entire life was to have a family. I had hungered for someone who I could love and who would love me in return. However, since my definition of love was grossly skewed at such a vulnerable age, I grew up with the belief that love was conditional. I believed love had to be earned and that it was dependent on one's actions, behavior and how they performed or obeyed. I believed that if a person did not comply with the expectations laid out before them, a complete thrashing of verbal and sometimes physical abuse would have to ensue. Past failures were thrown in the offender's face as though there was some imaginary record to review. If that were not enough, a physical beating would occur under the guise of love – love demonstrated and implemented through correction that is. Again, because I learned that love defined was selfish, demanding, unforgiving, easily offended, controlling and sometimes violent, I thought my actions were justified. I thought that because love fluctuated from one minute to the next and was conditional, it made it acceptable to abuse, criticize, belittle, and/or throw anyone, even my husband and children away when they no longer met or fulfilled my expectations of them. I believed that it was more advantageous for a person to walk away first than to take the chance of someone they "loved" to leave first. My definition of love was twisted, and I'm saddened to say that selfish, expecting, critical, demanding and abusive love was all I offered to my husband and children.

For years, I put them through hell on earth. I created daily an unsettled environment for them to live within. They never knew what they were going to come home to each day. Some days, I would be calm and compliant because I had had a peaceful and satisfying day. A day where I achieved all my goals to my idea of perfection. A day where I felt the emptiness within had been somewhat filled. However, in the early years, those days were few and far between. For the most part, my days were what I perceived to be far from perfect. I felt as though I was empty and in a perpetual state of loneliness. I was unsatisfied and unhappy with everything about my life. Every day I just wanted to run away! The way I dreamed my life would be once I found "love" seemed more like a nightmare to me. What is truly pathetic is there was no reason on this earth to feel that way. You see, as undeserving, blind and indifferent as I was in those days, God in His mercy and love had given me the most loving, giving and patient husband. A husband I had hoped for but was too blinded by the hurt and pain from my childhood to see. He had also given me four of the most beautiful, intelligent and loving children anyone could want. But alas, the problem was not them…it was ME! I just didn't realize it at the time. I thought they were the reason for my unhappiness. Therefore, I subconsciously did my best to make their lives as miserable as I could because I wanted them to suffer, too. I placed the same ridiculous, unobtainable expectations on them to perform that had been placed on me as a child and that I continued to place on myself. After all, true love was performance based, wasn't it? In any case, it was how, at least in my mind, I could ensure their love and devotion for me.

In the early years, I was determined that my children would be perfect. While they did their very best to do and be all I required out of them, it was never good enough. I did not allow for mistakes to be made. If they did make them, I was relentless! I treated them the same way I was treated as a child since that's what love did. Control was a huge issue as well. I had to have control over every aspect of their life. It was the only way I could guarantee our lives would be without blame, at least to all the on-lookers, and that I could ensure our home would be filled with "love." I didn't realize I was creating a perfect storm in our home. I didn't realize I was teaching my children to define love the same way I had been taught. I didn't realize they were growing up feeling just as unloved and rejected as I had felt.

My husband, on the other hand, is a phenomenon! To this day,

I don't know why he didn't leave me. Any other man would have left me a hundred times over. Even though he was married to an unstable, faithless, explosive woman, throughout the years he remained by my side. Day in and day out he showed me compassion, patience, understanding and a love that I could not comprehend. In fact, because I did not understand it, there were times that his response to me would only heighten my anger and rage. I was ruthless and abusive both verbally and physically to him as well. Yet, he remained calm and there for me. He never walked away. He never left. In fact, his love for me seemed to grow even deeper. I could not understand why he continued to stand by me. I thought something had to be wrong with a man that would not leave regardless of how hard he was being pushed to leave. Instead, my husband stayed, and my husband prayed! It was not until years later that I realized why...God had a plan (Jeremiah 29:11) and He was using him to help open my eyes and prepare my calloused heart to receive true love – God's love.

God's love for me always seemed incomprehensible. I heard about it when, on occasion, I went to church with my grandparents as a child. I heard about His love for me and His forgiveness of my sins. Yet, it never seemed to make a difference in my mind as to what love looked like or how I felt. Even though I did exactly what they told me to do (I repented of my sins and asked God into my heart), I continued to believe that His love for me was just like my earthly father's love – conditional! I believed that if I did not do something right, no matter how big or small or how important or insignificant, I would lose His love too and therefore, my rite of passage to heaven. I believed that I had to be perfect and work for His continual forgiveness and for my salvation. After all, I was told that I was *to work out my salvation with fear and trembling."*

(Philippians 2:12). Because I believed what I was told, I lived in a constant state of uncertainty and fear of losing it. Therefore, I believed each time I "blew it" - each time I failed to be perfect - I had to start my salvation walk all over again. I started over more times than I care to admit! This only perpetuated my internal misery. Oh, I put on a great front. I sang in the choir, taught Sunday school, held home Bible study and even played the Virgin Mary in the Christmas cantatas on more than one occasion. No one would have ever guessed that I believed I would never be good enough to achieve the perfection required to earn God's love. No one would have ever known that I thought I would never make it to heaven and that I was scared to death that I was destined to live an eternity in hell. For years, every time we sang the old hymn, "Jesus Is Coming Soon," fear would grip my heart! I just knew He would come at a time when I was not ready. To say the least, my thinking was warped but at the time I did not know it. All I knew was that I would never be good enough or perfect enough. It was my reality. It was my truth.

I was just about to give up and walk away when God revealed Himself to me in a way that I could not deny. I will never forget that night. The night that would change my life forever! I attended a church conference in Houston, Texas in the spring of 1981. The conference was held at what was then the Houston coliseum. I can still see where I sat when an evangelist spoke on knowing who we are in Christ. He said, "We were the righteousness of God through Christ Jesus" (II Corinthians 5:21). I had never heard that before! Oh yes, I had heard that Jesus died on the cross for the forgiveness of my sins. However, I had never heard that because Jesus took my sins upon His back, I was once and for all made acceptable to God and placed in a right standing relationship with Him by His gracious loving-kindness. Until that night, I had never heard that God's love was unconditional. I had never heard His love for me was patient and that it would never fail me (I Corinthians 13:4-8) and that His love kept no record of my wrongs…in fact, that He had thrown my sins "as far as the east is from the west" (Psalm 103:12) never to hold them against me again. Then, when I was told He would "never under any circumstance desert me or leave me without support or helpless" (Hebrews 13:5) and that nothing I could ever say or do would ever "separate me from the unlimited love of God, which is in Christ Jesus" (Romans 8:38-39), I was blown away! I found out I no longer had to work to be perfect to earn His love. I found out that He accepted me and loved me just for who I was with all my imperfections. There are no words to explain the overwhelming flood of emotions that gripped my heart and soul that night. I fell on my face and lied prostrate on the cold, sterile coliseum floor as I cried out to the Lord to forgive, heal, cleanse and redeem me unto His own! I remember when I got up from the floor, I felt that *"though my sins were as scarlet that He washed them as white as snow."* (Isaiah 1:18) I remember I cried all the way home and did not stop for three days. For the first time in my life, I felt clean! I felt free! I felt LOVED! Such a complete sense of joy flooded every part of my being. All I wanted to do was shout it to all who would listen that I was loved and accepted for who I was - just as I was! I no longer had to prove anything anymore to anyone, nor did I have to be perfect or work to be loved. For the first time in my life, I knew that I was loved with a love that had no conditions attached to it. I was consumed by His grace and mercy and love. Oh, the peace and sense of belonging I finally felt! For the first time in my life, I had a Father who loved me and who I knew would never abandon me.

Now you would think that the story would end there, "happily ever after," wouldn't you? You would also think that since that night, I would have lived out my life trouble free with a complete sense of contentment and "joy unspeakable and full of glory," wouldn't you? The truth is, while the Lord performed a major surgery in my life that night and I left the coliseum a "new creature in Christ" (II Corinthians 5:17), I had a massive amount of healing that still needed to take place in my mind and heart. You see, it was not until my heavenly Father's love became truth and life to me that I finally understood the kind of love, or lack thereof, my earthly father had for me. It was not until my eyes were opened to the depth of God's unconditional love for me that I realized I had put up walls of self-preservation since my early childhood to protect myself and keep others out.

Which brings me back to the beginning of my story – looking for that perfect shell that is hidden in the sand. Sometimes in the hunt only a fraction of a piece of shell may be sticking out of the sand and because that's all we see, we tend to pass it by. However, if we do decide to stop and give it a second look, we must take the time to pull back the layers of sand to uncover it to determine it's true worth and beauty. Sometimes we find only a broken shell, but sometimes we unearth the most beautiful shell of the day. I have found in my walk with the Lord, that He does the same with us. The big difference, however, He doesn't pass us by. We're not hidden from Him. He knows exactly where we are always. He doesn't have to dust off layers of sand to see us as worthy of his love. He already knows. His vision is twenty/twenty as to who we are with all our faults and imperfections and yet, He calls us worthy! He sees and knows the cry of our heart. He already knows what's under the layers of hurt and shame. He knows and sometimes, such as in my case, He takes the time with love and care to pull back each layer of pain and regret one at a time. As He does, He pours out His healing oil to "anoint and refresh us until our cup overflows." (Psalm 23:5 paraphrased). For that reason, all these years later, I am still a work in progress. The Lord, through His Holy Spirit, continues to "transform me into His image from glory to glory..." (II Corinthians 3:18 paraphrased). And because His mercy is new every morning and His grace continues to carry me through each day, I can honestly say, it is well with my soul! I can honestly say...

I AM LOVED UNCONDITIONALLY! (I Corinthians 13)

Have you walked through life feeling abandoned, rejected and alone? Have you spent every day of your life trying to be perfect because you desired to be accepted? Do you long to be loved? If you have answered, yes, to even one of these questions...reach out to Him today! He sees your tears and knows your needs! You are not hidden from Him. Reach out, take hold...He's there waiting patiently for you just as He waited for me! He loves you.

Soul Questions

- Have you or someone you love walked through life feeling abandoned, rejected and alone?

- How has this feeling of inadequacy played itself out in yours or your loved one's life?

- What is the one scripture from this chapter that brings you peace and comfort and reminds you of God's unconditional love for you?

You may contact Catherine at cwade.soulsinthesand.com and hewalkswithme.cwade@gmail.com
Facebook: hewalkswithme
Instagram: hewalkswithme cwade

Catherine Wade

Catherine Wade is a graduate of McNeese State University in Lake Charles Louisiana. She graduated Suma Cum Laude with a Bachelor of Art degree in Early Childhood and Elementary Education. She maintains teaching certifications in both Texas and Virginia as well as certification with the Association of Christian Schools International. Since graduating, she has taught all grade levels K-8; however the majority of her tenure has been teaching Pre-Algebra at the Middle School level where she feels called to teach. In addition, Catherine has held the office of principal, dean of women, chapel coordinator, praise and worship leader and curriculum advisor.

Teaching from the perspective of God's Word is Catherine's greatest passion. After years of struggling to figure life out on her own, her deepest desire to help others see that His Word is the only source they need to find healing, restoration, deliverance, comfort, hope, peace, joy and most of all love! Therefore, any subject Catherine is called upon to teach, she filters it through the Bible. Throughout the years, Catherine has taught and continues to teach in the classroom arena, as well lead numerous Bible studies in her home and teach at the annual ACSI Convention.

Catherine and her husband Bill reside in Lynchburg, Virginia. Together, they have four grown children and 13 grandchildren. During their free time, Catherine and Bill enjoy spending time with their family, leisurely walks in the evening, hiking, working out in the gym, traveling, and especially vacationing at the beach!

Chapter 4

Callings in the Sand

"Refreshed"

By Carol Thompson

The floor is cool to my feet as I head to the kitchen in the early darkness, flip the light switch, and begin to scribble the vivid details of the dream that jolted me awake.

I had been standing in front of a large metal trough filled with muddy water and green weed, like sea tangle that can wind around your ankles and trip you when wading out from the Gulf shore. The trough was filled with hundreds of red leather boots of all styles and sizes floating in the muck. The waterlogged boots, some decorated with fringe or silver medallions, were mud-stained and mismatched. I was fishing through the shoes, pulling on soggy boots, trying to find two in my size that matched. Once, I thought I had two of the same pair, only to see that both boots were on one of my feet, causing me to hobble around unevenly on the floor. I was frustrated and defeated in my attempt to calm down and find a "normal fit."

Fully awake, I began to "interpret" my dream. I live in Texas but had not put on a pair of boots since the 60s when I wore brown "hippie boots" and a pancho! A good friend has a red leather, boot-shaped coin purse for her Mah jongg quarters, but that didn't explain a whole cow trough of red boots. I pondered the hopelessness and anxiety I experienced during the dream.

I was "thirteen years out" from the September night my daughter, Sarah, died in a pedestrian hit-and-run in San Antonio, Texas. Her third year of law school had just begun when the ringing of the bedroom telephone startled our sleep. I heard the father of Sarah's law school roommate and dear sixth grade friend. "Carol, Sarah's been hit by a car and you and Ted need to get down there."

Before I could speak a single word or begin to comprehend the twists my life was taking, I was transported back, standing in our first home. Sarah, then about four years old, and I were having a routine conversation about something I don't recall. I said, "Well, when you get to be an old woman…" She looked up at me and said in a serious, knowing voice, "Oh, no, Mother (she always called me 'Mama') "I'll never be old." I assured her, of course she would be old someday, but I never forgot her words.

Standing beside the bed, phone in hand, a large white, flowing banner bearing its message in a bold cursive font, waved before my eyes. *"….and that's it…."* I knew Sarah was gone, that we would not arrive at the hospital to see our seriously injured child with any hope of life on earth pulsing within her. A choice presented itself to me at that moment. I would either run away from God or run toward him. I turned to the Holy Spirit.

Sarah's friend's dad offered to put us on a plane or to drive us, but we jumped into our car and took off. It was a tortured journey. Moving through the dark miles of the lonely East Texas highway, our car rumbled over a large armadillo that ran beneath the vehicle seconds after the headlights shined on the hard-shelled animal. It was a cruel and dreadful omen.

My heart knew that Sarah was no longer alive, though the words had never been spoken. I continued to stay in touch with Sarah's friends who were out with her that night, now holding vigil in the hospital, but no information was forthcoming. We made a quick stop at a fast-food restaurant where I again called the hospital. I was transferred through a string of nurses before the doctor came on the line. "We don't normally do this on the telephone," he said, "but I know you are driving and it's dangerous for you to rush." I sensed his compassion as he spoke. He told me they had worked very hard to save Sarah, but that she was gone. He told us to drive carefully, and I thanked him.

I delivered the devastating news to Ted as gently and as kindly as I could. "She's gone," I told him. I knew I was breaking his heart. His stunned expression told me he had continued to hold out hope. Two policemen walked past us on their way into the restaurant. "We just found out that our daughter was hit by a car and has died in San Antonio," I told them. They stared at us, said nothing and continued walking. I remember thinking, "poor training." I have no idea what I expected from them.

Ted and I made promises. No matter how bad things got, we would stay together and not divorce. We were aware of the dismal odds of making a marriage work after the death of a child. To make things worse, Ted's two-year-old daughter, one of three precious girls from his first marriage, had died decades earlier after being run over by a car on Halloween. I was sick at heart on many levels. I had been unable to fathom, and had inadequately acknowledged, the pain he carried all those years.

We continued through the darkness toward the city that had been a favorite vacation destination. We loved the markets, the River Walk, the food and culture of the people. I had remarked many times that visiting San Antonio was like enjoying a foreign country. The sun was rising over the downtown buildings as we arrived at the hospital and took our first steps into our new world. We began calling our loved ones and made the first of many decisions. "Yes, Sarah told me three weeks ago she wanted to be an organ donor," said her roommate. The next day the law school organized a poignant church service to memorialize Sarah and to support us. Still wearing the same clothes, we spoke with law enforcement and local reporters who were working to locate the vehicle and the driver who struck Sarah, missing two of her friends by inches, and then fled.

I had gone to bed the last night of Sarah's life a married woman with two grown stepdaughters living in Arkansas and Kansas with their families, and Sarah, who was 24. Ted, a career newspaper reporter and editor, and I married after meeting in the newsroom of the local newspaper. A few years later, I went to work for the federal courts where I was employed when Sarah died.

The morning of Sarah's funeral, I stood on our front porch in a state of disbelief, terror, and heightened senses. I took in every bloom of the wild purple vine, the slight change to cooler fall weather, with an intense revelation that nothing for me could ever be the same. I stood in front of the bathroom mirror, brushing my hair in a different direction. My recognition that I could no longer be the person I had been began that morning. I was lifted out of myself and left as a dry, empty tube. It would take many years for the replenishing to begin.

Psalm 121 distressed and comforted me at the same time. When Sarah moved from home, I had written a special "mom to daughter" letter which included the words of this divine psalm. The psalm was posted on her refrigerator. I took the psalm apart line by line, word by word, trying to figure out from my human perspective what had gone wrong. "He will not let your foot slip - The Lord watches over you - the sun will not harm you by day, nor the moon by night - The Lord will keep you from all harm - he will watch over your life." I visualized over and over my beautiful, spunky, former high school point guard, hurling ninety feet up toward the late summer moon. I gave my Psalm 121 fears, doubts and confusion a title. "Seeking Heavenly Answers to Earthly Questions."

I was obsessed with figuring out at what point Sarah could no longer breathe. I wanted to believe she was immediately unconscious with no pain and suffering. I felt heavy pressure in my chest at night and slept propped on two pillows, so I was able to breathe. I self-analyzed that if Sarah could not breathe, then neither could I. The twenty-four years of life I lived with Sarah now included her loss of breath.

Growing up cushioned by a loving Christian family and special friendships, I could have never imagined the unfolding events. I could not comprehend the sudden physical separation from Sarah. Where was she? In my limited thinking, she was somewhere, but I could not name the "where." I was fearful and realized my total lack of control. God had what I wanted - my daughter. What if I could not "get there?" Even more torturous for me, what if Sarah did not "get there?" My mind was racked with worry every waking moment. My greatest fear was living to be old. I faked through my anger when well-meaning people said, "you will probably live a long life like your mother." I was screaming inside, "that is the worst thing you can say to me."

I never thought Christian believers carry a guarantee from the world's problems and tragedies, but I was overwhelmed. A pastor said, "When we are taken to a difficult place, we listen more to God." Never have I so diligently "searched the scriptures." I collected Bible verses of faith and comfort and taped them to green index cards. "Be strong and courageous. Do not be afraid; do not be discouraged, for the Lord your God will be with you wherever you go." Once, in the darkest hours of the night, I fell as deeply into anguish and hopelessness as I will ever go, lying in silence and stillness, coming face to face with the presence of the Holy Spirit. I mark the moment I began moving upward toward healing. Psalm 18:19 and 2 Samuel 22:20 provide verses for what I experienced. *"He brought me out into a spacious place; he rescued me because he delighted in me."* The anxiety and airless claustrophobia began to lift. Years later, when my pastor said in a sermon that "salvation" means "bring to an open place," his words fell into my grateful ears.

We Need Not Walk Alone is the online magazine and motto of The Compassionate Friends, the international support group for families grieving the loss of a child or children. Soon after Sarah's death, at the urging of one of my mother's friends whose daughter had died in a car accident, I became a participant in our local chapter and found Thomas Jefferson's loving and thoughtful quote to be one of the great truths of my new world. "Who then can so softly bind up the wound of another as he who has felt the same wound himself?" The Compassionate Friends provided a place to plop down among friends, share tears, funny memories, bitterness, anger, and laughter. The monthly meetings gave moms and dads the opportunity to speak without discomfort the names of their sons and daughters who had passed, and encouragement to survive.

Compassionate Friends was, and is, a wooded pasture of hundreds of twinkling fireflies, or lightning bugs as we called them as kids. One friend glows with positivity and "bright hope for tomorrow," providing a guiding light in and out of the dark woods for the others.

If that friend dims with the day's discouragement, another steps up to shine words of love and life.

The second Christmas after Sarah's death, my mother set aside holiday traditions, and treated us to a Caribbean cruise out of Galveston. One morning we joined passengers who signed up for an island excursion to swim in the sea and relax in the white sand. Ignoring the water's chilly temperature, I ventured out. I warmed up, dropping to cover my shoulders. Except for one man who was swimming, the other passengers remained on the beach. I bounced around, soaking in the solitude, a speck on the earth surrounded by God's gigantic waters. When I came closer to the man in the water, I spoke, and we traded stories. He was mourning the death of his father and had taken the cruise for a change of scenery. Expressing my condolences, I told my story, that we were trying to "get away" from the sorrow of losing Sarah. The man was quiet, and then he told me he worked as an emergency room nurse at the hospital Sarah was taken the night she passed. He had not been on duty but knew the circumstances of her death. We stood together in the water, learning that even though it is impossible to outrun pain, God places people together, even strangers, to comfort one another. "You are not alone in this. I will pray for you."

"God gives us life-changing knowledge." I sat in the stain-glassed chapel during Wednesday Midweek Meditation and felt the pastor's words slip right into my heart. Sarah's death cracked me open like a piece of the "broken pottery" in Psalm 31:12. God provided the mortar to reform my brokenness into a different mosaic, a new piece of pottery to be placed with fresh insight and responsibility wherever God wanted me.

One Sunday my pastor posed a question during his sermon. What six words would you want to be engraved on your tombstone? I e-mailed my answer to him that afternoon. *Blessed To Share A Friend's Pain.* Grief birthed empathy and compassion, a desire to connect with those who have suffered a loss and are trying to figure out how to "do the next thing." What if, I thought, no one was called to be a counselor, nurse, dentist, hospice worker, ambulance driver or funeral director because, well, there will be unpleasantness and discomfort? It's the same with grief; difficult, painful, awkward. Who hasn't ducked the grocery store aisle, gone into avoidance mode, changed the subject? We utter well-meaning platitudes, ask thoughtless questions. Are you *still* grieving? I learned to take a breath and walk across the room to begin a conversation. "I heard you lost someone precious to you and I'm sorry. I've had you and your family on my mind."

One afternoon it was my turn to talk with callers who dialed our local Compassionate Friends helpline. A call came from a father in another state who was deeply concerned about his son's distraught state of mind. His son's child, the caller's grandchild, had passed away in our area. The meeting I arranged with the grieving father turned into several hours of tearful conversation standing outside of a grocery store. I trusted God to oversee the outcome, knowing my role was to be a listening, encouraging companion. When we prayerfully attempt to provide assurance to others, Luke 12:12 promises *"the Holy Spirit will teach you at that time what you should say."*

Ted and I devised a code to give each other a pass, calm things down when anger, despair, and misery brought us to speak rudely or critically to one another. "Is it Sarah Sad?" we would ask. Ted, with his history of heart problems, looked at me one evening and said, "I don't have enough years to live to get over this." Less than three years after Sarah's death, Ted fell dead in our home as we were getting ready to go out for Chinese food with close friends who arrived moments after. Picturing Ted and Sarah standing together in the heavens consoled me. I knew Ted "deserved" his own mourning, but several years went by before I could "separate" my grief for Ted from my grief for Sarah. I buzzed around in a blur, moving from one activity to the next.

"I have heard you calling in the night." A calling, by one definition, is an impulse toward a course of action "accompanied by conviction of divine influence." I am confident in my calling to encourage and reassure others, share my collection of Bible verses, my rescue through God's grace and mercy. I experience freedom in the words of Psalm 40:2. "He lifted me out of the slimy pit, out of the mud and mire; he set my feet on a rock and gave me a firm place to stand." Grieving parents from every country, creed and culture in our world share spiritual kinship. 1 Corinthians 12:13 tells us, *"For we were all baptized by one Spirit into one body - whether Jews or Greeks, slave or free - and we were all given the one Spirit to drink."* Validation of grief is essential for healing. Sharing stories, confiding emotions and the events surrounding a grief is a sacred trust, bubbling up from the deepest part of a human being.

"I lift my eyes to the mountains....my help comes from the Lord." Comfort from Psalm 121. When waves of grief and trauma rolled higher and deeper, I pushed to the surface for air. The anticipation of the "wave" - Sarah's birthday, the anniversary of her death, a holiday, the change of seasons - was often more difficult than the event. The Lord provided family and friends, supportive co-workers, pastors and church friends, my walking companions,

writing and mah jongg groups, my counselor of ten years, and Sarah's cherished friends. People who stayed when I was no fun to be around. I learned to calm myself reading towers of books by Anne Tyler, C. S. Lewis, and everything in between. Author Henri J.M. Nouwen, my spiritual companion, is available to me between the covers of his books. I create opportunity to rest in quiet solitude. "Be still and know that I am God."

I bought thank-you notes printed with Proverbs 11:25. *"Whoever refreshes others will be refreshed."* One friend sent a work-of-art fruit bouquet when Ted passed. We wandered in and out of the dining room munching cool, green melon and plucking juicy strawberries; refreshed. Preparing food for my family and friends is who I am. I am calm and content baking desserts for Sweets for the Soul, my church's hospice ministry, or feeding visitors seeking refuge from hurricanes. I love being a cog in our local "bus stop water cooler" project. My Stephen Ministry training describes caring for others as "offering a cup of cold water." GriefShare demonstrates ways to provide and receive healing, how to "encourage one another and build each other up." Refreshed.

I grew up with family who love to visit the cemetery and often took me with them. So, I am at peace wandering among the monuments, stopping to read names and dates and details. Sarah's beautiful Bahama, or Mystic Blue, stone is inscribed with carefully chosen Bible verses and precious sentiments. Her stone has a characteristic that I have never seen in another monument. On rainy days or when I rinse dust off the stone, the inscriptions on both sides disappear, leaving a cool, smooth surface. When the stone dries, the words reappear. I love this peculiarity in her stone. I think of Sarah's baptism day, Ted's baptism in a country creek, and of the washing away of my own sins. Sarah's "blank stone" encourages me. Revelation 21:4 reminds me. "He will wipe every tear from their eyes. There will be no more death or mourning or crying or pain, for the old order of things has passed away."

"Whatever is lovely, whatever is admirable - if anything is excellent or praiseworthy - think about such things."

I prayed for my mind would calm down, direct my focus to Sarah's twenty-four years instead of the night she died. Whatever is good and true. Today, I think of Sarah's laughter, her joy and love for her family and her friends, people she met along the way. I see her face, beautiful from the moment she was born to the last time I held her before she backed out of our driveway to return to school. I rest in memory of her sweetness and humor, her competitive nature, her mischievousness and love of a good time. I think on her strong spirit, "someone so gentle and so kind," wrote one young man, her appetite for adventure and homemade potato soup. Our little spark moved quickly through her years, accomplishing much, loving much. The clack of her heels coming through the door on the wood floors stirred things up and brought life. Sarah's Song is my sacred silence.

Driving to a recent poetry conference, I passed two signs hammered to fence posts miles apart. Since neither sign was associated with a restaurant or other stop, I accepted them as guideposts from thoughtful people communicating with passersby like me. "Wander Far," said one sign. "Travelers, Take A Break" read the second. Thirteen years after Sarah's death, I learned that Psalm 121 is known both as, A Prayer for Travelers, and, The

Traveler's Psalm. The Psalm gives me an eternal perspective, traveling one continuous journey rather than dividing my earthly life and my future eternal life into separate sections. "The Lord will watch over your coming and going both now and forevermore."

The "boots in the water" dream intrigues rather than distresses me. With Holy Spirit guidance, I am on my forward road. When I fall behind, or sadness becomes my shadow, I usually recover quickly. I trust Sarah and Ted's safekeeping, and my own, to the words on Sarah's confirmation plaque. *"And surely I am with you always, to the very end of the age." Matthew 28:20.*

We are told to not worry about tomorrow as each day has enough trouble of its own. I have no idea where my next steps will take me. Whether I wear red boots or flip-flops, Isaiah 30:21 will speak to me. "Whether you turn to the right or to the left, your ears will hear a voice behind you, saying, "This is the way; walk in it."

"When peace, like a river, attendeth my way,

when sorrows like sea billows roll;

whatever my lot, thou hast taught me to say,

It is well, it is well, with my soul."

Soul Questions:

- What images come to mind when you see or hear the word "refreshed?"

- "Let me get you something to eat, so you can be refreshed and then go on your way," reads Genesis 18:5. Recall a time a friend or relative provided special refreshment for you.

- What ways to provide refreshment to others does the story suggest?

Carol may be contacted at

cjpt@suddenlink.net

Carol Thompson

Carol Thompson, retired federal court employee and former newspaper reporter, writes poetry and articles. She began the rebuilding of her life, and the examination of her spirituality as a Christian woman, after the death of her daughter, followed by her husband's death three years later. She contributes to anthologies and to organizational and church publications. Carol has been published in The Compassionate Friends *We Need Not Walk Alone* and National Public Radio's (NPR) *Marketplace.* She describes her life as "walking a road I've never been on before," and finds contentment in writing about the everyday aspects of growing with grief after the death of a beloved child. She enjoys cooking for family and friends, browsing bookstores and attending writers' conferences. Carol strives to respond to her Holy Spirit calling to share her experience and "no-platitudes-encouragement" with those close to her, and in service to the "angels unawares" God privileges her to meet.

Chapter 5

Souls in the Sand

"Courage"

By Lisa Pulliam

Silence was heavy in the car as we drove the two hours from our home to the airport. As dusk of a November evening fell upon us, I glanced his way and wondered, "What are we doing? Who is this man I am married to? I don't even know him anymore, and he doesn't know me…."

We were headed to celebrate our 25th wedding anniversary with a weeklong tropical Caribbean vacation, just the two of us: no church meetings, no business seminars, no kids, no agenda. When was the last time we had taken a vacation like this? Our getaways consisted of business combined with pleasure: meetings, breakout sessions, networking. And if our vacations didn't involve work, they involved children, a different kind of work. But this trip was none of those. This trip would be Chris and me and nothing to do. No agenda, no meetings, no alarm clock, and no cell phones. As we drove these silent miles, a feeling of guilt startled my thoughts, "I don't even want to go on this vacation with him…. What are we going to talk about? What do we even have in common anymore? I have work to do back home, a business to build, money to be made. I don't have time for five days of nothingness with a man who is almost a stranger…"

The plane was only half full, so we nestled in for a four-hour flight with an empty seat between us. Chris pulled out a book out and started reading. I took my journal and a pen out of my bag. I was secretly relieved to be alone for a little while on a vacation that was meant for two. As the plane sped down the runway, I leaned back, closed my eyes, and whispered a prayer, "Dear Lord, please protect us in flight, keep our children safe while we are away, and somehow, someway, help us find our marriage again." I let my hair fall down the right side of my face to hide the tears that began to flow. I opened my journal and wrote, "Lord, what has happened to my marriage? What has happened to my life? I don't know if I am coming or going. My business is doing well, but I am not. Something is out of balance. I feel like I am standing on one side of the Grand Canyon and he is standing on the other."

As our airplane carried us to our anniversary destination, my thoughts and tears transported me to a soulful search into the life I had been living over the past few years. My journal became a net, capturing my heart's concerns, fears, and longings. I thought about the difficult family situations we had walked through the previous year, the first one a pea-sized lump on the front of my neck I had noticed in the bathroom mirror one evening. Weeks of doctors' appointments, biopsies, and tests brought news that it was a benign thyroid nodule, which, I was told, could wreak havoc on my body in the months and years to follow if left untreated.

As I took shaky steps down the path of my health situation, a second storm hit out of nowhere. It arrived in the form of a call from the headmaster at my son's private high school asking us to come for a meeting in his office. An hour later, we sat in silence as the headmaster informed us that our son was in trouble. A nightmare was unfolding before our eyes. He had made a poor decision which would not only cost him his starting position on the Varsity basketball team his upcoming senior year, but more than that, a place in this top-notch school. In utter disbelief, we stood up and walked out of the school with our son. In my first book, "Toes in the Sand", I wrote in depth about the journey we took with our son through this difficult situation.

One year later, I was on an airplane traveling to celebrate a marriage that had been put on the back burner of my life and was now suffering for lack of time and attention…a marriage I questioned. Would it, could it last much longer? Only time would tell.

In my world, the ocean is magical. I am not a morning person, but at the beach, I am simply unable to sleep in. The magnificence of God's creation all around me causes my internal alarm to wake me earlier than I ever wake up back home. In fact, my eyes usually pop open while it is still dark outside. The sound of the waves rolling onto the shore is like a voice from heaven beckoning me to come, savor and enjoy.

Sure enough, the first morning of our Caribbean vacation, I found myself wide awake in the dark wondering what time it was. Was it 2:00 am or 5:30 am? Is it safe to walk along the beach in the middle of the night in a foreign country? How much longer until sunrise? I fumbled for my glasses and phone… 4:38 am. With daybreak nearly two hours away and unable to go back to sleep, I got up, grabbed my Bible and journal, and sat at the little table in our room, continuing my conversation with God by the light of my cell phone flashlight. Every few minutes I glanced out the window anxiously awaiting the first glimmer of morning light.

Around 6:00 am, it was time. I slipped on my shorts, t-shirt and flip flops, and whispered a prayer asking for protection as I started to the beach alone. Chris was still breathing heavily enjoying his good night's rest. *I'm glad one of us will get some sleep on this vacation,* I chuckled to myself as I stepped out the door of the hotel and followed the path toward the beach.

Have you ever experienced the feeling of soft wet sand between your toes in the early morning hours? Ahhhhhh, it's one of my favorite sensations. An orange glow was just beginning to color the horizon as I made my way slowly down the beach. The smell of the salty sea air and the sound of the ocean waves rolling onto the shore were familiar to me and brought a soothing balm to my restless soul. As the tall palm trees waved good morning to me, I noticed myself breathing ever so slowly and deeply as if thoroughly exhaling all the hurt, the disappointments, and fears of the future and inhaling all that was beautiful and majestic and good in this scene unfolding before me. Light on the horizon ahead reminded me that the sun would soon be rising.

"Creator of this beautiful world," I whispered, my steps sinking into cool, sugary sand, the sun's rays illuminating the crystal blue water, "I feel like I have strayed from You and the plans you have for me. In the quest for my identity over the past few years, somehow, I have lost myself. How is that possible? Please help me see my life more clearly. I have goals, dreams, plans, and desires, and I have been working so hard to accomplish them. I thought I was doing what you called me to do. Thank you for giving me the opportunity to be an entrepreneur and achieve the success I have had so far, but the rest of my life feels out of balance along with everything and everyone important to me. I am seven years into my career. I have had my eyes on the prize of success, yet why do I feel empty and sad?"

I was empty. My soul was running on fumes. I didn't know where I was headed, but I was speeding 90 miles an hour to get there. For the past year, I had been dealing with my health issue, with many more questions than answers and no solutions that I was comfortable with. We had walked with our teenage son through his challenges and he was emerging a strong and resilient young man. But with health challenges looming, and a marriage that was in quick sand, I needed to stop struggling, be still, and grasp onto something more stable.

At that moment, as if God Himself highlighted that realization about my life, the sun lifted from the ocean to greet the new day. I stood captivated by its beauty. "Lord, I am here, and I am open to You. Help me, please. Show me what to do and I will do it."

The acknowledgement that something is wrong is always the first step towards healing and wholeness. Being aware of and facing the fact that there is a problem takes humility and taking steps to make the changes necessary requires a boatload of courage. Humility had been missing in my life. It was his fault our marriage was sinking. I was working hard to contribute financially to cover for all the money he wasn't making. Sure, he was always supportive of my business venture, but he didn't understand why I had to be gone so often attending meetings, trainings, on conference calls and up late at night sending emails. How many times over the years had he stopped by the door of my home office to ask me when I was coming to bed? My answer was usually, "I have lots to do tonight… you go on to bed and I'll see you in the morning." A slight forced smile and shoulders down, he would kiss me goodnight, then turn to leave me to finish my work.

At the time of this 25th anniversary vacation, we had one preteen, one teenager, and two in college. The financial pressures in our home and family were weighing us down as if we were swimming across the ocean wearing backpacks full of rocks. For 18 years my husband had been the sole provider for our family of two, then three, then four, five and now six. He worked hard and was passionate about his calling as a pastor. While Chris carried the financial responsibility for our family, I enjoyed being a stay at home mom. When I stepped into my new business seven years before, life around the Pulliam house changed dramatically. At first, I was energized by learning to be an entrepreneur. I enjoyed the people, the challenges, and the opportunity to develop my skills in marketing, speaking and training. I enjoyed the personal development, becoming a leader, and contributing financially for the first time. And quite honestly, I enjoyed time away, being my own person, creating an identity apart from just wife and mom, and becoming a respected leader in my company.

Working longer hours, staying up late, getting up earlier, and being gone from home more had become the new normal. My family, mainly Chris, was getting the leftovers these days, and I don't mean leftover food! The "leftovers" of me, my energy, my smile, my love, my attention. Leftovers were pretty much all I had to offer.

Speaking of food, I had always enjoyed cooking and serving my family healthy meals, but those had become few and far between in this new life I was leading. Now we were eating quick meals on the run. Chris had taken up extra duties such as going to the grocery store and doing more of the cooking, or rather, "food preparation". Most meals came out of a can or a frozen bag these days.

On the beach that first morning, as the sun illuminated a fresh new day opening before me, my heart was illuminated with an assurance that a grander plan was unfolding – one of which I was only beginning to get a glimpse. And I knew in that moment this trip away with Chris was divinely inspired. It was as if the Lord of Creation Himself had plucked me right out of my busy life, put us on an airplane together, and plopped us down on a remote island

2000 miles away! Yes, He even made sure there was no internet connection! It was as if He had things to tell me and had not been able to get my attention. But here, in this breathtaking oasis, He had my full attention. My soul felt an assurance that if I would trust Him, humble myself, face the truth about my life, and admit that my priorities had been misaligned, that this could be the turning point for which I longed. It was as if He were speaking to my soul, "I have never left you, and everything is going to be alright. The sun is rising in your life, Lisa. Keep your eyes on Me and trust Me."

Over the days that followed, with our souls in the sand, Chris and I talked again, laughed, cried, prayed, admitted fears and failures, laughed some more, and asked forgiveness when needed. We celebrated the recent news that our daughter and son-in-law were expecting their first baby. We were going to become grandparents the following summer! We took a catamaran ride, went snorkeling in the vast aquarium of the Caribbean and tried parasailing for the first time ever soaring high above the brilliant teal waters. We danced and watched sunrises and sunsets that took our breath away. I felt the layers of emptiness, uncertainty, and selfishness peel away. A sense of peace I had not felt in years returned to my soul.

That was two years ago. Now I sit here at home, writing this chapter, and feeling an overwhelming sense of gratitude for that pivotal time in my life. I returned home with a new clarity and a renewed commitment to live life differently than before. Our tropical anniversary vacation had brought me much needed rest and reconnection with myself, my husband and my Creator. Having my toes in the sand had opened my eyes to new possibilities, ideas, and a future without fear. I was back in more ways than one and it was time to make changes in my life and priorities. Traveling down the same path I had been on was not an option anymore.

One of my favorite thought leaders, teachers, and entrepreneurs is Mr. Jim Rohn. I have listened to him and learned from him for years. One of his greatest lessons came to me during this time:

It's not what happens to you that determines your life's future. It's what you do about what happens. All of us are in a little sailboat. And it's not the blowing of the wind that determines your destination, it's the set of the sail.

The same wind blows on us all. The wind of disaster, the wind of opportunity, the wind of change. The wind when it's upside down, the wind when it's favorable, and unfavorable. The economic wind, the social wind, the political wind. The same wind blows on us all. The difference in where you arrive in one year, three years, or five years is not in the blowing of the wind. It's in the set of the sail.

I had been blaming the direction my boat was sailing on the winds around me and failing to realize that my sail needed adjusting! It was time for me to reset my sail and steer my boat in a new direction with my priorities of God's calling on my life, my family, and then business. But where to begin? When I examined my daily schedule and time management, I realized many little decisions and actions needed to be changed. I would catch new, fresh winds, and steer my boat in the direction of the life to which God was calling me: a life of gratitude, special times with my family, inspiring others, living courageously, and embracing habits of good health.

As I made small adjustments in my life to my sail, I was reminded of the scripture, *"You will seek Me and find Me, when you seek Me with all your heart." Jeremiah 29:13*

And so, I did. I looked for Him and trusted Him to show me the steps to take in adjusting my sail. The top two priorities were apparent: my personal health and my family. They missed me, and I missed them.

My thyroid nodule was a lingering issue as I had been dissatisfied with the medical advice I had been given months before by my endocrinologist. She had recommended either surgery to remove my thyroid or killing the function of my thyroid with radioactive iodine. Both options would cause me to rely on synthetic thyroid medication for the rest of my life. I am not a "medication person". Deep down in my gut, I knew there had to be another way to deal with this issue. What had caused this nodule to grow in the first place? I had always considered myself a healthy person, seldom running through the fast food line, and trying to eat salads as often as I could. If anything, I didn't stop to eat often enough, and probably drank way too much coffee throughout the day running from appointment to appointment. But I had no typical symptoms of someone with a thyroid imbalance.

When it comes to health, I am a firm believer in the human body's capacity to heal itself using natural remedies whenever possible. So, in my newfound mission to dig to the root of this issue, I consulted my sister, a registered dietician, who had access to trustworthy information on thyroid disease. And guess what we quickly found to be the main cause of thyroid and other autoimmune diseases? Yes, you guessed it. STRESS. Who, me? Stressed out??? WHAT DO YOU MEAN I AM STRESSED OUT???!!!

Guess what causes stress? Not enough sleep, toxins in our environment, food, skin care, cleaning products, inadequate nutrition, too much caffeine, running on empty, not taking care of oneself, increased financial obligations, an exhausting work schedule... the list goes on and on. My research and introspection were verifying some revelations from my time in the sand. The fast-paced lifestyle of the previous few years was not only taking its toll on my marriage, but on my health as well. I was learning that true health is all intertwined: body, mind, soul and spirit, almost like the four legs of a chair. When one is off balance or hurting or missing, the whole person is affected. Good health is a treasured gift we have been given, and I had taken mine for granted.

Isn't self-awareness powerful? It requires us to eat a big piece of humble pie (coconut cream pie, please), face reality, and begin to courageously shift the sail of our boat so we can catch the winds in a more favorable direction...and that is exactly what I did. With the help of a local holistic doctor who specializes in autoimmune diseases, along with the guidance of my sister as my nutrition advisor, we set a plan in place for me to proactively take control of my personal health again. Instead of midnight and beyond, my new bedtime became 10:30 pm. Instead of meetings and conference calls every night of the week, I stayed home more, shut the computer down, and drew new boundaries between business and personal time. When I felt anxious about what others would think about my new priorities and a newfound word in my vocabulary, "No", I would remember Proverbs 3:5-6, *"Trust in the Lord with all your heart and lean not on your own understanding. In all thy ways acknowledge Him and He will make your paths straight."*

With my sister's help, I began to cook healthy meals, incorporating a "paleo" diet, lots of veggies, lean meats and healthy fats, into my lifestyle. I began taking nutritional supplements and using essential oils. Instead of rushing out the door to meetings every night, I enjoyed lingering over dinner with the family and lively conversations, cell phones in another room. I cut down on coffee (oh how I enjoy my coffee!) and started drinking more water. I realized that rest was as important as air to the human body, mind, soul and spirit. Chris and I went on date nights again to our favorite Mexican restaurant, leisurely visits to my favorite local winery called Kiepersol, on a Saturday afternoon, and evening walks. I realized life is a gift and God has given me one shot at this thing called life. He created and gave me this body and I better take care of it. After all, if we don't truly love and care for ourselves, how can we possibly love others with grace and joy, as He intended for us to do? How can we possibly be all He created us to be?

Have you ever thought about how it's the little things in life that truly make a difference? It's the small adjustment of the sail that steers the boat toward the desired destination, like an unhurried hug and kiss, offering a loved one your attention and full eye contact, being quick to notice and affirm something your child or spouse does well while resisting the urge to criticize or nag, surprising your teenager with bacon and eggs for breakfast, jumping up when the alarm clock rings to take an early morning walk instead of pressing the snooze button again, taking time to pray, writing a thank you note, expressing gratitude throughout the day, smiling and saying hello to the person in line at the grocery store, cleaning out your spouse's car... just because. The "little things" may include not making that spontaneous purchase and instead choosing to honor your spouse by sticking with the family budget. Truly, it is the little things in life that make a huge difference.

Sometime later, I was attending a marketing seminar with a mentor of mine, Kimberly Pitts, when I had an "ah-ha" moment. You know the kind I'm talking about, some call it a divine tap on the shoulder. These moments seemed to be happening more frequently as I was slowing down and listening more intently. God's still small voice seemed to whisper to my soul once again, "Lisa, I have given you creativity, passion for life, and a great capacity to love, inspire and encourage others. Lisa, don't you see? All of this is from Me. I created you. I knit you together in your mother's womb. You are fearfully and wonderfully made, Lisa. I know that because I made you. And all I have made is beautiful. Now go and encourage other women who are weary in life, whose marriages are drowning, whose careers have overtaken their lives, or who just need time to rest and reconnect with Me and other like-minded women who are open to My voice in their lives. Take them to the place where you most powerfully feel My presence, experience My magnificent creation, and hear My quiet voice in the salty sea air and brilliant sunrises over the ocean."

In that moment, the Toes in the Sand Women's Retreat, an annual three-day retreat on some of the most beautiful beaches in the country, was born. This retreat offers a time of rest, connection, laughter, and inspiration among women who arrive as strangers, and leave as sisters. I am deeply grateful for the opportunity to share life with the incredible women of courage who bring open hearts, vastly different journeys, and deeply similar longings to this event. My prayer is that those who attend will never quite be the same. And guess what? I will never be the same. I have a calling on my life that is greater than me, bigger than any company, greater than any amount of material wealth, and more thrilling than any level of personal success or recognition. It's called purpose.

Do you find yourself asking, "What is my next step, Lord? What is my purpose? I have asked those question a thousand times. In an interview I heard recently with best-selling author Barbara Brown Taylor, she shares a story of an encounter as she asked those same questions of the Lord. In her book, *An Altar In the World* , Barbara says, "One night when my whole heart was open to hearing from God, I asked Him what I was supposed to do with my life. God said, 'Anything that pleases you.' 'What?' I said, resorting to words again. 'What kind of an answer is that?' 'Do anything that pleases you', the voice in my head said again, 'and belong to Me.'"

Guess what? The God of the oceans and sunrises and palm trees and the cool morning sand that brings a smile to my face and joy to my heart… that same God created you and loves you with an everlasting love. He already knows what pleases you. He knows the plans He has for you. He knit you together in your mother's womb. You are fearfully and wonderfully made. You are His. He loves you. Rest in this love and step into the woman He created you to be.

"For you created my inmost being;

You knit me together in my mother's womb.

I praise you because I am fearfully and wonderfully made;

Your works are wonderful, I know that full well.

Psalm 139:13-14

Soul Questions

- I have been learning to take better care of myself and the body God gave me. I enjoy walking, journaling, eating healthy, drinking more water and less coffee, listening to inspiring music, crawling into bed earlier each night, date nights with my husband, and of course, putting my toes in the sand whenever possible. What are some ways you relieve stress, slow down and put yourself as a priority?

- It's the little things in life that can make the biggest difference. Have you ever acknowledged that your sail needs adjusting? If so, write down three adjustments that you can implement today which will shift the sail of your life in a new direction.

- The definition of Courage is "the ability to do something that frightens one; strength in the face of pain or grief." What is ONE courageous step you would like to take in your life? In your marriage? With your children? In your career? In striving for balance between work and family? In your community, church or world around you?

Lisa would love to keep in touch with you and hear your story. You may contact her at lisacarolpulliam@gmail.com or visit her website at www.stepwithlisa.com

Lisa Pulliam

 Lisa Pulliam is a woman on a mission to live a courageous and impactful Life. She embraces her enthusiastic purpose to inspire women to face fears, overcome their past, and realize who they were created to be. But it hasn't always been this way.

For 16 years Lisa's work as a Domestic Engineer was at home and in church. As a stay at home mom of four children and a pastor's wife, Lisa set her career aside and concentrated on becoming the best mom, wife, and ministry volunteer she could be. Family life transitioned when Lisa's husband Chris accepted a position as Senior Minister of a church in Texas. It was during this time that Lisa sensed a deep restlessness in her soul. Something was missing. While she valued the life she had, Lisa knew she was meant to do and be more.

Lisa launched her own business in 2009 in the direct sales industry. Her entrepreneurial spirit along with her teachable spirit allowed her to achieve the second highest leadership level in her company, Executive Consultant. This experience provided tremendous opportunities for personal development and learning how to empower others to succeed. She learned skills such as making effective phone calls to potential clients, developing and leading a marketing team, and presenting and training in front of a group. During this journey Lisa realized she had a passion for speaking.

Along the way, Lisa had the opportunity to realize a dream: She finished her book that had been in the works for years: *Toes in the Sand, My Journey from Domestic Engineer to Entrepreneur.* Now a published author, Lisa embarked on a new journey of impacting women's lives through speaking, writing and hosting her annual *Toes in the Sand Women's* Retreats, which she holds at beaches across the country. In her spare time, she enjoys spending time with her family and her precious granddaughter Emma.

Chapter 6

Stuck in the Sand

"Overcoming"

By Trish Holt

Oh my Gosh… What just happened? Did he just do that? What did he just say? What did I say that made him do that? This is crazy. I can't believe it's happening again. I'm so embarrassed and ashamed.

I was sitting at my favorite slot machine oblivious to what was happening around me, I was focused on the spinning wheels lining up the winning payout, dreaming obviously, when suddenly, my boyfriend was calling me names and accusing me of sleeping with the guy sitting several machines over. I had never seen the other man before, had not spoken a word to him but somehow, I was intimate with him?! This was crazy! Who was this person in my life and why was this happening? It's like the devil just transformed into my boyfriend right before my eyes.

I found myself trying to explain that it wasn't true, I hadn't even spoken to this stranger, but he just kept getting more verbal and out of control. I finally convinced him to leave. As we drove back to the hotel I tried to control my every breath as to become invisible and prayed we would get back quickly without another incident and he would just pass out.

As we walked into our hotel room, he threw me onto the bed and started to choke me. I thought at that moment this was it, I was going to die. I knew not to fight back because that only made him angrier, so I didn't say a word. I was lifeless. He opened the second-floor window and was trying to throw me out. He told me, "Your family won't even be able to recognize you when I am done". There was a swimming pool directly below us, so I knew if I just hit the pool I would survive. The visions of missing it never came to mind; instead I started thinking of my son Austin who had died 8 days after he was born 16 years before. He has always been my Guardian

Angel. The night after he was born I was so sick, close to death, from an infection with high fever. Suddenly, my hospital room was filled with Angels! The beautiful white glow of them circling around my bed is indescribable. I remember being outside my body, floating with them before falling into a deep sleep. I awoke the next morning free of fever and infection. Suddenly I was brought back to reality as I struggled to breathe but I could hear God's whisper…." I got you, be still, and be calm". The peaceful assurance that no matter what happened, GOD had me was my only comfort. I could picture Angels around me now and I knew it was almost over. Then to my surprise, and relief, he let go of me, crawled into bed and passed out.

I should have run at that moment and stayed away. I had left before but always came back because of my job and since it was hours away from my home state, I would fall right back into the relationship with him. I had dreamed of achieving this position in my career and I wasn't giving it up for anyone. I loved what I did, loved traveling and helping build other salons, but that was an excuse for the real reason. I kept telling myself I wasn't strong enough, mentally or physically, to get away and stay away. I tried to figure out what I was doing to make him go crazy, and I must admit, I'm a lot like my dad…. I had to try to prove to him it wasn't me. It was him. I would settle for what and where I was at that moment and try to look like everything was wonderful. I was living inside an egg shell, trying not to breathe and break it. My boat was stuck in the sand and every time I tried to make it to water, I would give up and give in.

The physical abuse didn't start the day I met him. He was charming and fun…I was new to the area and only knew a couple of people so having someone show me the town and places to go was exciting for a while. Then the gentle controlling started…not wanting me to go back home to see my friends and family, always needing to be around me, calling constantly to see what I was up to, showing up at my work because he missed me. Then it progressed to breaking the car window out instead of hitting me, even wrecking the car by trying to run us off the road. He threw cell phones out the window and keys in the lake. After trying several times to move and him finding me, I realized the only way out was to quit my job and move back home. Home was in another state, so that bond with him would be broken forever.

With God's grace I finally broke away from that relationship and moved on with my life, never stopping to work on myself. Just a new start, in a new city, with no one that really knew me or the baggage I brought. That had always been my solution because I never took the time to find who I was and heal from all the pain I carried. Do you see a pattern here? I've been in this boat for years, stuck in the sand going nowhere.

I decided a couple of years ago that I wanted to share my story with other women who might be going thru the same thing, so I started writing. It would be about my journey of living through physical abuse for 5 years. The title would be "How I met the Devil and Fell into Hell"! Great title, right? As I was writing I came to the realization that he and I were both fighting demons in our minds and he only acted that way when he was drinking. He really was a good person until the alcohol took over.

The demons in my mind started a long time ago, as a child. I had experienced situations that made me start questioning myself and who I was. What is love? What do I believe? Am I ever going to be worthy of God's love? Is it a sin to do this or isn't it? Will I ever be good enough? What am I? Who am I? The list goes on and on. I had been experienced years of verbal and emotional abuse from being called names like "Trasha"(instead of Trisha), "Stupid", and "Wabash" (big butt I guess), to not having any emotional or physical contact the whole time I was pregnant. Those demons in my mind kept coming back. I didn't deserve love or affection; I wasn't good enough for him. I had a life of looking for love, support and affection from the wrong type of people for all the wrong reasons, but more importantly, I didn't know what it was really supposed to be in the first place.

Year and years of building a wall around myself, I was the best in the world at playing the "got it all together" game. I looked, talked and walked like everything in my life was wonderful, but when I looked in the mirror…oh what I saw. On the outside I looked successful, but was living paycheck to paycheck, filing for bankruptcy twice; I was in an intimate relationship, being verbally, emotionally and physically abused; I cared about other people, yet I smiled and walked away from conversations as fast as I could. I couldn't and wouldn't let my guard down or let people get too close because I didn't want them to know the real me and what a failure I really was, inside and out. I was screaming for help in my heart.

So, I found a new career, grew fast within the company, but deep inside I longed for more. I started network marketing in my spare time and began meeting like-minded people. My vision and dreams started returning. I have always loved to travel, see new parts of the world, try new adventures and experience all types of cultures. I had enjoyed doing those things with my previous career in the hair salon industry and growing up my father would take us on summer vacations to as many states as we could travel in a 2-week time frame, but I had also always wondered what my purpose was here on earth. What would my legacy be?

My heart needed the networking community where I found myself longing for the positive friendships and mentoring. I found true friends with this company and started to surround myself with encouraging, focused, ambitious women. Women that believed in me, accepted me and loved me. It was a God send and I found my walls start to slowly crumble. It was still hard to let them get too close. I kept them at hearts bay. Just in case. That business never exploded. It was just on and off, on and off, that's how I worked it. Those friendships, however, have exploded into lifelong relationships and introduced me to my current passion, a company with a vision and desire to change the world through acts of kindness, by sending cards and gifts. I love this idea so much but talk about a foreign language! How could I express caring about someone and mean it? I had struggled with this my whole life! I started sending thank you cards to my customers, to friends and mentors. Then for birthdays, anniversaries, accomplishments, graduations and on and on. First it was kind of hard. There's a saying "Pretend that you like someone and pretty soon you will." Pretty soon you will begin to make a connection in your own mind and then the connection will grow with others. Wow, that was still tough for me. It was still hard to let people in too close, but as I continued to send I felt a change going on within me. I was touching other lives and it started to feel good. In the past, when people showed me love and compliments I accepted them as half -hearted because I felt I didn't deserve them. I was unworthy of any type of praise, but this started opening up my heart and allowing me to see the good in others and myself.

Then I went to one of the company trainings and heard, "The stories of your mind become the stories of your Life" (Kody Bateman, Chief Visionary Officer SendOutCards). Kody tells a story of the tennis ball and his dog. And how when he throws out the tennis ball his dog runs to pick it up and bring it back to him to throw again and again, no matter how dirty and slobbery it gets. When Kody gets a new clean ball to throw, the dog is reluctant to let go of the old slimy one he has in his mouth to pick up the new, clean one. This is an example of us not letting go of the old dirty, slimy, crap we have in our minds and in our lives to go for the new, clean possibly life changing and prosperous future because we are scared.

As I pictured this dog, hanging onto that slimy, dirty, nasty tennis ball, I saw myself hanging onto the thoughts in my mind and how I felt about myself. All the years I had attracted the negative, hurtful relationships and how I was unworthy of the new me. The stories of your mind become the stories of your life. The stories of your mind become the stories of your life! WOW! It was like Kody was talking directly to me. Now stories of your mind can either be positive or negative right? For me they were on the negative side.

The profound moment was when Kody did an exercise called "I AM STATEMENTS." Now I have set goals and New Year's resolutions and given up on them after about a month, but to write down I AM STATEMENTS was new to me. I had never heard of that. An "I AM statement" is a form of an Affirmation statement starting with I AM. Affirmations are positive statements that describe a desired situation and are repeated many times to impress the subconscious mind and trigger it into a positive action. To ensure the effectiveness of the affirmations, they must be repeated with attention, conviction, interest and desire. Unfortunately, too often, we repeat negative statements in our minds without even being aware of what we are doing. Your subconscious mind accepts as true what you keep saying, and eventually attracts corresponding events and situations into your life, whether they are good or bad for us. So why don't we choose positive statements? It's our choice.

I wanted to become invisible because I couldn't write anything down. All I could think about was I AM NOT. I put down a couple of I AM's just, so no one would notice I didn't have any. Then 6 months later I went to another company training and heard Kody speak and train on the same topics. This time I couldn't hide anymore. I have known for years that if my life was going to change I had to change, and my life wouldn't change unless I took the first step and started. It wasn't about what had happened to me or who had done it, it was about who I wanted to become. Until you are ready for the process it's just words. I had to deal with that person I saw in the mirror. I felt the tears swell up in my eyes as I wrote down I AM NOT'S. I couldn't say or think I AM until I dealt with I AM NOT'S. They just started rolling out of my head onto the paper. I AM NOT WORTHY, I AM NOT BEAUTIFUL, I AM NOT STRONG. I AM NOT LOVEABLE! I had said them in my mind so many times. When I finished the I AM NOT's, I turned the paper over and wrote every one of them as I AM's, even though I didn't feel or believe them YET.

I AM BEAUTIFUL, I AM SMART, I AM SEXY, I AM WORTHY, I AM SUCCESSFUL, I AM HAPPY, I AM LOVEABLE, I AM BLESSED, I AM CARING, I AM STRONG, I AM POSITIVE, I AM BRAVE, I AM RICH

Remember the definition above about affirmations or I AM statements? They must be repeated with attention, conviction, interest and desire. I started saying these to myself every morning in the bathroom mirror as I got ready for work. I started to see a change. I started to believe in that person looking back at me and I started to like her. She was good, beautiful and worthy.

I went to the national conference 2 months later and here are some of my new I AM STATEMENTS! I AM AN AUTHOR, I AM AN EAGLE, I AM STRONG – MENTALLY AND PHYSICALLY, I AM HAPPY, I AM A SPEAKER, I INSPIRE THE ABUSED, I AM ENJOYING THE HOME OF MY DREAMS ON THE BEACH, I AM FINANCIALLY FREE, I LOVE MY LIFE, I HAVE A SUCCESSFUL RANCH FOR SPEACIAL NEEDS CHILDREN AND THEIR FAMILIES, I ATTRACT LIKE MINDED PEOPLE AND I AM CONNECTING THE WORLD WITH KINDNESS

Now some of these have not come true yet, but for the first time in my life I know they will because I AM changing. I do have something to contribute to this world and to others!

No matter what you feel inside take the time to write it down. The negative, the hurts, anger and pain you feel. Forgiving and letting go of the who, the why, and the how is the only way to ever find true healing. Then make yourself turn them around to positive I AM STATEMENTS. Even if it sounds crazy, do it! You will be surprised at what it does to your mind, and what your mind starts to see, your heart starts to follow and feel.

I must thank my dear friend, confidant and mentor Lisa Pulliam. I remember praying that we would become friends because I knew she would make me a better person. We laugh about this now because I had no idea what Lisa was going thru in her own life. Her journey of finding out what she wanted and needed to do, but God has such a sense of humor and he had this planned all along. A friendship that can't be put into words. Thru her, God's plan is taking me to more than I could have imagined. I never dreamed of speaking at the Toes in the Sand Women's Retreat much less help plan them or getting to write a chapter and speak about my journey, wanting to help other people. Be careful what you pray for. No really! I wouldn't change any of it because now I am realizing my purpose and what I can leave behind.

My journey is just beginning, and I pray that wherever you are in your journey…not started, just begun or traveling, you will find the "I AM" within you and start writing new stories in your mind and heart.

Aspire to share that with all of us for we all have demons in our minds of some kind, chapters of our lives that can inspire someone…I just pray mine has touched you in some way.

"The stories of your mind, become the stories of your life" by Kody Bateman means positive stories now…not the past negative ones.

Soul Questions

- What slimy, dirty tennis balls are you holding onto (what negative thoughts, I AM NOT'S or beliefs about yourself are keeping you stuck)?

- What story in your mind has created a chapter in your life?

- Write down 5 "I AM" Statements about Yourself.

You can reach out to Trish at trish.soulsinthesand@yahoo.com or visit her website at www.trishholt.soulsinthesand.com

Please send a FREE heartfelt card to someone at www.trishholt.com

Trish Holt

Trish Holt is a Native Texan, growing up in the small town of Brownsboro. She currently works as a full time corporate benefits and wellness leader, but Trish has always been an entrepreneur at heart. She opened her own hair salon in 1985, and eventually launched her own business in the direct sales industry. But underneath her confident smile, Trish struggled for value and self-worth and this inner struggle created "demons" in her mind that created the stories of her life. Behind the facade of a happy life, Trish endured a series of abusive relationships: verbally, mentally and physically. Her life began to change when she found "I AM statements" and a passion to bring people together through relationship marketing and acts of kindness. Trish loves the outdoors where she can reflect on God's beautiful creation, but the beach is where her heart desires to be.

Chapter 7

Lighthouse: Illuminating Light Through the Storm

"Illuminate"

By Regina Burdett

The hallway was long, cold and echoed as I walked down it. Everything was familiar and foreign at the same time. This was the hospital where I worked but this time I was the patient. The nurse asked if I needed to be with someone and I told her no thank you. With tears running down my face, I darted into the first restroom I found. I tried to catch my breath over my pounding heart, wiped my tears, and waited long enough to ensure that there were no more people in the waiting room of the clinic. As I walked out, my most challenging task was still ahead of me. I had to drive home and tell my husband, Doug, that our unborn, first child had medical issues and the doctors were not sure exactly what kind.

My drive home felt like I was in a tunnel. Due to the tears, I could not see anything in my peripheral vision. It was a total blur. I could only see the road directly in front of my car. This forty-minute drive home felt like I was driving on a large treadmill. The road under me was just rotating and it felt as if I was not moving forward. What do I say to Doug?

I spend my days working as a child life specialist, teaching and playing with children so they can learn about and cope with their medical experiences. This conversation should be a piece of cake, right? Doug had expressed, years earlier, that he was not sure how well he would cope having a child who required a routine life of doctor appointments, surgeries or hospitalizations. I assured him that though I see these kinds of things every day, the odds are small. But on that day the odds were 100% that our child would be living a life of doctor appointments, surgeries and hospitalizations. That is, if he survived birth. There was a huge unknown of what was exactly happening. This was the conversation set before me as I left the hospital. I had to tell him that his worst concern is now our reality.

Doug and I were high school sweethearts. I know how strong he really is, because he puts up with me. Years ago, when he expressed his concerns of not being sure he could be a strong dad for a child with medical needs, I knew he had what it takes. He is compassionate and loves with a big heart. Now, I had to help him see that in himself, while, at the same time, questioning myself. What was God thinking?

I believed I did not have what it takes to be a full-time working mother of a child with medical needs. I also knew the statistics, that fifty percent of marriages end in divorce, when the family has a child with lifelong medical needs. I have seen it play out in the families whom I serve in the hospital. I was completely terrified. I could not do this alone. I needed Doug by my side. He would need to scrape me off the floor at some point, I was certain of it.

I am not exactly sure how I did it because I was very shaky as I sat in the driveway. I reminded myself of three things before walking into our home. God is always with me. I have a loving husband who always supports me. Doug and God will not abandon me. I pushed my fear way down into the pit of my stomach, slowly walked into our home and began the conversation I was dreading.

The basic information was that the baby was not swallowing, the heart was rotated while positioned all the way to right side of the chest and part of the lung tissue did not look like it was functional. This caused me to retain high volumes of amniotic fluid. My belly was bigger than it should be seven months into my pregnancy. This symptom could cause pre-term labor. The doctors' three main goals at this point were to monitor the baby, learn more about his condition and prevent me from going into pre-term labor. Doug was so calm on the outside. His arms just wrapped me up and pulled me close, so close that I could feel his heart beating. He was not shaking like me. As he took in deep calming breaths, I was certain that he was experiencing the same whirlwind storm of thoughts and emotions as I was that evening. I remembered eating dinner and sitting on the couch watching TV. We were looking at the TV, but we were not focusing on the show.

This was the beginning of a long storm for us.

So, you may wonder why this chapter is entitled Lighthouse. Well, a lighthouse is a tall structure with a high-powered lantern at the top. They are placed along the shoreline. Their purpose is to illuminate the shore and waters so that a ship captain can safely navigate during storms and times of impossible visibility. It protects the boats as they move forward on their path toward their destination. To the lighthouse keeper and community, the lighthouse represents their commitment to protecting life, providing security and safety. Our storm needed light to guide us. Where was I going to find a "life" lighthouse? It was not as simple as driving down to a shoreline and lighting up the lantern.

Doug was and continues to be my lighthouse. I knew he was traveling on the same journey with me, but he has a way of calming me down. Just his presence alone brings me comforting assurance. Have you ever been in a moment where chaos is swirling around you, mentally dizzy and so confused that your muscles do not even know what to do next? All you want to do is fall to the ground in the fetal position? I felt that way during the remaining two months of my pregnancy.

I had weekly doctor's appointments with the neonatologist, a special doctor for women having high risk pregnancies. The team performed many tests on me and the baby. It was terrifying knowing so much information and at the same time no idea what was really going to happen after the birth.

Doug was at my side for every procedure. The first time they needed to tap me, to remove some of the amniotic fluid, it was not planned. I was just visiting the neonatologist and after the ultrasound he said we needed to do the procedure. Doug was over an hour away at work. The biggest risk of the procedure was going into pre-term labor and that made me very anxious. As my heart pounded, I asked if we could wait for a few hours so that Doug could be with me. The doctor agreed to wait, and I called Doug immediately.

This was not a simple task because I could not reach him directly. After three phone calls, I finally got to hear his voice. He was calm and confident that he would be there within an hour. That hour, however, felt like two or three as I was moved to the procedure room and watched the nurses bring out all the equipment. Everything was in slow motion and yet it was happening so fast. I wanted everything to stop until I had Doug at my side. The nurses attempted small talk, but I was praying for Doug to have a speedy and safe trip. Every time the door of the room opened I popped my head up, in hopes that it was Doug walking in. Nothing at that moment meant anything to me until the door opened and I heard the nurse say, "There is your hubby". Doug was rushing in and yet had the best smile on his face. He lit up the room and I could feel my anxiety melting away.

I went through the procedure holding his hand. I chose not to watch. At my job, I coached kids through the same kind of procedure to remove abdominal fluid. I knew that a long needle would be inserted through my skin, through the wall of my uterus and a large syringe would be used to remove fluid. This time was different because it was in the uterus versus the abdominal space. If the fluid was removed too quickly I would have a contraction that could lead to labor. It had to be done slowly and it was an absolute necessity that I remain relaxed. A muscle cannot be relaxed and contracted at the same time.

Control over my own muscles was a key factor in preventing contractions. I had this image in my head and I had chosen not to watch. Instead, I gazed into my husband's face. The room was dark, to allow the doctor to view the ultra-sound screen clearly, but Doug's face was lit up by the light from that screen. He held my hand just tight enough that I could feel his calm muscles and not too hard to feel fear. The doctor began to show Doug things about the baby. I could see joyful glimpses of smiles as he saw our baby moving around. Quickly, that smile became a look of shock. He tried to hide it, but the frozen face muscles along with the intense stare told me a different story. I could hear a quick gasp throughout the room. Everyone became silent and all movement came to a halt.

I gave a quick squeeze of Doug's hand and asked what was happening. My doctor described to me that the baby had reached out toward the needle and grabbed a hold of it. Horrified that the baby would get hurt, everyone stopped moving. I kept my eyes on Doug. Finally, his face relaxed, and he looked back at me. The baby had let go of the needle and went back to moving around. A long sigh of relief was let out by everyone. That was the moment that I knew we were going to make it through whatever was still ahead of us.

We had to get right in the face of fear and do nothing except wait - on God.

As we all know, there are two main reactions to fear: fight or flight. God showed me at that moment that the fight was on. He gave me the strength, calmness, and love through this one man.

Two months of these kinds of experiences were just the training I needed before giving birth. I can say this now, looking back. In those moments, I was on a rollercoaster ride of baby showers, baby shopping, selecting a name, weekly doctor appointments, test results and one more tapping of the amniotic fluid.

Several weeks later, we got a call from our close friends from college that their second child was born. They lived in the same town and our due dates were only 4 days apart. Rachel had arrived. I was huge by this point and my due date was still 2 weeks away. We went to the hospital to meet Rachel and I resolved to hold her that day, no matter how I felt. The doors in the hallway of the hospital were decorated with baby wreaths announcing, "It's a Girl" or "It's a Boy". The cheerful colors of pink, blue, and white were radiant, the sounds of laughter filled the hallway, staff were excitedly scurrying around, and joy floated in the air. I was on a mission to find their room and hold my goddaughter. Shortly after arriving, she began to wake up. She curled up her legs, wiggled her face and began to cry. Her dad changed her diaper, wrapped her up in a blanket and began to walk with her. He was so exhausted and yet the smile on his face glowed. Despite all of this, she still cried. I offered to help by holding her. My secret mission was implemented!

I had her in my arms, slightly bouncing her as I walked the room, and she calmed down. I was in hog heaven. She gazed at me for a few moments and then fell asleep. It was hard for me to breathe while holding her, but there was no way I was putting her down. I could feel her little legs, arms, and the wiggles of her head as she snuggled into my chest. Then I began to hope that soon I would be doing this with my baby. My fear was that I would not get to and Rachel became my surrogate baby.

Four days after Rachel arrived our son was born. We named him Benjamin. That day was not what I expected, and yet, it was. Will he be fine? Will I get to hold him? Will he live or what? Right before I gave my last push, my neonatologist popped up over me and said, "If the baby cries right away I will let you hold him for a few moments but if he does not, I will hold him up for you to see and then take the baby out to get care." That exact moment I screamed quietly, inside in my head, that I was not ready. But I had no choice. He was delivered, did not cry, and I only got a brief look at him. I told Doug to follow the doctor out of the room to be with our son. My doctor returned to care for me as we waited to hear if he would begin to cry right outside of the delivery room. Finally, he did, and boy was he loud! The door was pushed open and the they held him up for me to get a quick peek before they rushed him off to the Infant Specialty Care Unit.

I did not get to see him again until the next day. That night he was evaluated and then rushed off to surgery. The surgeon visited us in my room to explain what he needed, and a nursery nurse gave us a picture of him. That is all we had to hold onto. The final diagnosis was Congenital Diaphragmatic Hernia (CDH) and a

Tracheoesophageal Fistula (T-E Fistula). Three months later he came home for the first time. Our life of tube feedings, weekly therapy sessions, doctor appointments and surgeries were just beginning.

Like any other life journey there are turning points in how a person reacts to events. One of those times was when our son was around 2 years old and hospitalized to work with a feeding team. It was safe for him to attempt eating, but it was not a natural, instinctive behavior. He had no idea what to do with fluids and food in his mouth. The g-tube allowed him to get the needed nutrition, but he had horrible reflux. We would feed him and within a few minutes most of it was coming right back up. Eating was not enjoyable, and he had no desire to participate. To be honest, I felt like a failure as a mother. Each meal felt like a torture session and I was inflicting the torture! What loving mother does that? Me! The mother who desperately wanted her son to be healthy, happy and tube free. This was a time of darkness I never thought I would personally experience. I was depressed.

I found a national support group for families who have children with one of his birth defects. During a conversation with another mom, I got a very clear picture of what my son felt like when trying to eat. Her daughter said to imagine lying flat on your back, you have someone shake up a bottle of soda and then put it in your mouth. There is an explosive rush of soda shooting out of the bottle and into your mouth. The out of control feeling, while attempting to swallow during that rush, is how trying to eat a small bite of food is for a person who does not have the muscle control to keep the food from going straight down the throat, before chewing. After hearing this description, I had a whole new respect and compassion for what my son was attempting. Her daughter shined a bright light on this part of our journey. Thank goodness for those who have traveled this journey before me and for the medical team willing to embark on such terrifying therapy.

Logically, we knew it was only in our son's best interest to go through this, but our hearts were pierced with agony as we forced him 3 times a day to put food in his mouth, to learn how to chew, move food safely around his mouth and to swallow. I would be down the hall from the session room and could hear him scream, hear sounds of physical struggles as he would try to push everyone away and then the football stadium cheers when he would finally take a bite that was small enough to fit on the tip of my finger. He would be brought back to the room, red in the face and his entire body covered in sweat as if he just ran a marathon. The moment he would make eye contact with me, I would see the look on his face, "mom please take me away from these people". His arms would fly open and he would have a death grip around my neck. That one conversation from that mom about her daughter carried me through ten more years of therapy to teach Benjamin to eat. This lighthouse was critical at the time we crossed paths.

Keep in mind that his team consisted of my co-workers, since Benjamin was treated at the same hospital where I worked. One member of that team was a psychologist who specialized in family counseling. I distinctly remember one visit she made during this hospitalization. She sat next to me, looked me square in the face and asked "Just how are you doing all of this? You work by day, work with Benjamin during your lunch break, you visit with the team and you are staying here overnight. Yet, you are positive and appear to have it all together. How?" I quickly popped her bubble.

I told her that there are many evenings that I lay in the hospital parent bed with my back to Benjamin's crib and the door of the room so that I could not be seen crying. I hurt so much watching what Benjamin must endure. Then, when I feel like I am about to throw my hands up, I think about all the people that my mom, family members and friends have praying for us. Since they are from all around the world, I realized that at any time of the day and night, someone is praying or thinking about us. So, who am I to give up now? The thought that someone is thinking about us every hour is very powerful and calming. I close my eyes to envision a person taking a moment to pause and think or pray for us. I get a blanket of comfort that covers me. At that moment I feel my breathing slowing down, my face relaxing and I just feel secure.

God is with me.

I made the choice to pull strength from others. Strength is the light that they illuminate. It is unconditional, ever flowing and always there. Since they were not being exposed to our life daily, they had what we needed. The strength a person has is not something a person can shut down. They may not realize that they have it, they may not utilize it all, but it is seen by others around them. Yes, many of my lighthouses did not know me, but as I heard their messages through family and friends, I could feel their desire for God to bring knowledge to the medical team, rest for Doug and myself, endurance for Benjamin and patience for all of us. Because they believed that God has a plan for our little boy, I chose to adopt the depth of their belief. That gave me the strength to do things for Benjamin and watch the things he had to go through, so that he could accomplish what was waiting for him in the future. I got knocked down many times. By choosing to bask in the light from the many lighthouses God created, it gave me the push to get up again. It was intentional!

I could have sat during despair, depression, and anxiety of overwhelming odds. Remember, I had two choices: fight or flight. You have the same two choices when faced with challenges. Which will you choose? Realize you are not alone in your fight. I had many lighthouses that our time here does not allow me to share with you. You might be asking, where are your lighthouses? You may think that you do not have anyone in your corner or that they do not have strength to illuminate in your journey.

I am here to say, yes you do!

Even if it is only the authors in this book, you have lighthouses all around you. You must make choices, with purposeful action, to find them or to be aware when one is placed in your life. Some of mine were already in place, just waiting to be utilized. Some I found during my challenge. God put into motion the relationships of our family, co-workers, neighbors, friends and friends of everyone we knew. God made sure we had a family friend first, whose newborn was a lighthouse for our entire journey, Rachel.

Now I am far along in this journey of being Benjamin's mom, where I can tell you he is thriving and tube free. He does most things like others his age. With every accomplishment, with every smile he gives, every time he realizes just how much he has accomplished and every time I look back at that first photo, I well up with a ton of emotions. Each emotion represents my love for Benjamin, my gratitude for my lighthouses and excitement of what is yet to come. The journey is not done, far from it, but I know that I am farther along than some parents who have children with medical needs. My survival through this storm, places me on the shoreline as a lighthouse. I choose to illuminate for anyone in need of my light.

When the time comes, will you illuminate for another?

John

"I am the light of the world. Whoever follows me will never walk in darkness, but will have the light of life"

Soul Questions

- Have you looked around to find your lighthouses? Remember they may be people who are mainstays in your life, people just now coming into your life and some may be those who crossed your path for only a moment but their impact on you is permanent. List them here to increase your awareness of their presence.

- When you are faced with challenges, what are the traits needed that you feel you do not possess? Take a moment to write them down. Then look at your list from the first question to see who possesses the traits you need.

- Have you asked God to walk along side of you in this journey? He is already there with you, but by asking you are being intentional which opens your heart to what God will provide for you. He can illuminate those lighthouses in your path who have the traits you seek, but you must be ready to see them. Use this space to write out a simple prayer to personally invite Him to be with you.

My journey is not finished. I have learned how to navigate the special/deaf education systems and currently guiding him in the transition to adulthood. I thank God for placing people in my life to lean on them during this time in our family. I love connecting with others and I welcome anyone who would like to contact me. You may reach me at ReginaBurdett.soulsinthesand.com

Regina Jeanne' Burdett

Regina Burdett married her high school sweetheart, Doug, after graduating from the University of Texas in 1989 and they have two sons, Benjamin and Nolan. As a mom, Regina has navigated the school system to advocate for her son, who has special needs. She and her husband founded an organization called PASSHI, Parent Advocates for Successful Students with Hearing Impairments. This group advocated for change and support for the local day school program in their area which serves over 100 students that reside in 10 different school districts. Their efforts resulted in students now attending schools which naturally feed each other versus attending three different school districts by the time they graduate. This has significantly increased the number of students being able to participate in extracurricular activities offered by the district, to develop lifelong childhood friendships outside of the day school program, to have continuity in the school curriculum system, and allows for the more efficient use of the school resources and staff.

Professionally, Regina has spent her life improving the lives of children. She became a Certified Child Life Specialist in 1994. As a child life specialist, Regina has served on several committees at the national level and is published in the book "Music Therapy with Hospitalized Children: A Creative Arts Child Life Approach". In 2018, the Texas Children's Hospital Child Life Department established the "Regina Burdett Award for Clinical Excellence" as an annual award to recognize child life therapists for clinical excellence.

In 2010, Regina began a new journey as an entrepreneur. Since becoming an entrepreneur she has gained a new perspective on personal development, becoming a servant leader and working alongside others who desire to create significance. Along the way, Regina has excelled as a presenter, trainer and mentor to those around her and the voyage is just beginning.

Chapter 8

I Used to Laugh

"Reclamation"

By Kimber Spinks

We all have friends who have those Etsy-ish "word signs" in their houses. You know the ones ---"Let your passion be your paycheck", or, "In this house we do forgiveness, do-overs, compassion..." All of these are inspiring words of wisdom to be sure, but another of my friend's "word signs" wins. Hands down. Every time. *"I laughed 'til tears ran down my legs!"*

I love that! Isn't it the best? Those words bring me images of laughing with wild abandon, no matter who is watching. The kind of laughter the Bible mentions numerous times: *"He will fill your mouth with laughter and your lips with shouts of joy! (Job 8:21)* That kind of laughter and joy should be one of life's goals, right?

I used to live in this world. Sing, have joy, be in love, be silly. I used to laugh like that. Laugh with wild abandon. Laugh in a way that would make many people double over. Only I didn't double over. My knees would buckle and down I would go. My closest friends were aware of this quirky characteristic and would rush to my side to hold me up before I fell. And hold me up they did. But more on that later.

Author Madeleine L 'Engle wrote, "A good laugh heals a lot of hurts". Mark Twain wrote, "Against the assault of laughter, nothing can stand". But what happens when Herman Melville's "mighty good laugh" becomes "rather too scarce a good thing"? When life has dealt you such a blow that even talking seems superfluous. When you scarcely have the energy to take a breath much less have a deep belly laugh. And even if you could muster the energy, you have no desire because nothing, *absolutely nothing,* is funny.

In June of 2016 I was dealt such a blow. I had already survived a precancerous and ultimate removal of my thyroid, breast cancer, broken elbows (yes, plural, and at the same time. Just get a good mental image of all the things I couldn't do with *two* arms in slings!), and a painful divorce after 21 years of marriage. I come from a family of very strong women and this strength carried me through to a point. But nothing could have prepared or strengthened me to withstand what was about to happen. Dark Times were coming.

Before the Dark Times I laughed a lot. My girls had been cracking me up since they became sentient humans. When they were about four and six, the Older of the two would ask her sister to tell her "that joke" again. It went something like this: "Why did the car/chicken/food cross the road? To drive/lay an egg/eat!!!" Hilarious, right?

"That joke" was different every time and made absolutely no sense but the Younger couldn't get the whole joke out before the Older was laughing hysterically! All the Younger had to do was start the sentence and the Older would dissolve into peals of laughter which of course would make me laugh because what Mama doesn't adore the sound of her precious daughters laughing together?

Carolyn Birmingham says, "A smile starts on the lips, a grin spreads to the eyes, a chuckle comes from the belly; but a good laugh bursts forth from the soul, overflows, and bubbles all around". This Good Laugh reigned supreme in our house, the music that played through our days, our nights, our years.

Don't get me wrong. It wasn't always rosy. Those sweet babies eventually became teenagers and all that laughter somehow dissolved into tears. Because, well, teenagers! But in time we found our big-girl panties and were able to find things to laugh at together again. Mostly our own weird selves!

From birth, my girls were always quirky and silly - and weird - but in really good ways. Mostly in ways that they would never want me to share in these pages (or anywhere else in life for that matter) but in ways that we could tease each other about and no one would get their feelings hurt. They were weird in ways that gave us inside jokes and "remember when?" stories to tell as they got older. My girls were beautiful, intelligent, deeply feeling, creative, and...WEIRD! That is my favorite characteristic to describe them. And truth be told, to describe myself as well. We are a weird family. To quote my beloved cousin with especially special needs, "Tooooo Weird!". (Abby, you are tooooo right!)

Weird is good, unpredictable, fun. It's a part of being in this world, living this wild and wonderful life. But this wild and wonderful life comes with no guarantees. No one asks to be born. Nevertheless, you are born. And I must believe that parents, people, do the best they can do with the tools they have at the time. So, one day you become a parent. But you happen to have an awesome set of tools! You absolutely LOVE this whole parenting thing! You dress them up warmly, you send them to school. You feed them organic food, make sure they get enough sleep, exercise, and cognitive stimulation. You give up your world to make sure their world is full of Girl Scouts, gymnastics, art camp, summer camp, piano lessons, guitar lessons, soccer, volleyball, basketball, track, and whatever else their inquisitive minds want to tackle. You feel good about this whole parenting thing. You aren't going to be one of "those" parents. You think you're killing it but all you are really doing is the-best-you-can-do-with-the-tools-you-have-at-the-time.

So, you are in your groove (that whole parenting thing and all). Life is awesome. You are loving your wild and wonderful life (no guarantees…).

And then you get a call-

... *"wait, what was that?"*

... *"what are you saying?"*

... *"Yes, I'm her mom! Is she ok?"*

... *"No ma'am, she's not"* ...

No ma'am she's not?

The Dark Times had come.

And then the words - So many words!

Accident, severe, life-flight, brain, lacerations, grim, (no guarantees…) broken, ventilator, call anyone?

Those were all words I knew. I knew their definitions. I had used them in sentences. And somewhere in my brain I knew their ramifications. But how could I make my brain understand what they all meant regarding my precious, sweet baby? My baby who had just graduated high school, my baby who exactly one week ago turned 18, my baby who had just spent the last four days with her sister, her best friend, getting a foretaste of the college life that she would, in less than three short months, be experiencing herself.

It was her first "road trip". She was on her way home and I

couldn't wait to see her. I called to tell her what I was cooking for dinner, all her favorites. I told her I loved her. I later called back to tell her... but I knew. In my gut I knew. How could I not? She was one of two humans in this entire world who had grown inside my body, had been absolutely one with me, flesh of my flesh. We were connected.

The dark times had come.

The wheels of her car on the driver's side had dropped off the shoulder. She overcorrected which caused her car to roll over twice, become airborne, and ultimately leave the roadway. Thankfully, the accident was witnessed by other drivers who called 911.

Whoever you are, I thank God for you for being where I could not be. She was not alone.

The first Good Samaritan on the scene found her breathing but not otherwise responsive. She was intubated by first responders and life-flighted to Mother Frances Hospital (where she was born) in her hometown of Tyler, Texas. When she arrived, she was in a coma, had broken ribs and deep lacerations on her upper arm and calf, as well as other cuts and bruises. Remarkably, other than a couple of lacerations on her chin, her beautiful face was relatively unmarred. She looked almost perfect, but the MRI revealed a traumatic brain injury.

And so, my precious Kendall was admitted on a ventilator to the Medical Intensive Care Unit.

The day of the accident a friend's physician husband was on call in the ER. "Can I call your friends?" "Please, yes" were all the words I could manage. One was driving home from Dallas, one from

College Station, one was in town and was there before I could even understand myself where I was. I couldn't get in touch with my older daughter, away at college. She was out on a run. But my friends found her friends who found her and drove her home. On that terrible day when the Dark Times came, a beautiful, loving, supportive Village began to assemble themselves around us. We were trapped within the four walls of room 121 in the MICU. But outside those four walls prayers were said, food appeared, un-verbalized needs were met, hands held me up when I could not stand on my own. There is not a minute I can remember in those awful five days in that hospital when a priest from my church was not there ministering to me, my family, and all the members of the Village, who had literally camped out in the waiting room for the duration. A spontaneous prayer vigil was held in the hospital's chapel and three more were held at our church, my girls' school, and the park. #prayforkendall started making its way around the world via social media. Pictures were shared, and words of support posted. There was only one set of footprints in the sand - God was carrying us.

I was dizzy from the roller coaster ride we were on during that time. My girl was silently, wordlessly, motionlessly fighting. She received medicinal cocktail after cocktail with ingredients I couldn't pronounce. We moved from words that I couldn't make sense of two numbers that I couldn't make sense of. Five at 12:22, 29 at 1:06, 14.6 of 50 mL/hr, green 55, white 13, yellow 121, pink... and on and on. All I could do was trust that the people dressed in blue and maroon and black understood this foreign language.

But those four walls. Damn those four walls that were holding my child prisoner. At first, they seemed so perfect, symmetrical. I trusted, *believed,* they would hold everything in place. But I soon sensed they weren't what they appeared to be. I could not see (did not want to see?) the crumbling, failing structure behind the façade. Scaffolding had been erected to try to maintain the integrity of the walls so that they could continue to hold everything in place. But the scaffolding was not meant to be permanent. And underneath the scaffolding the walls continued to crumble. And the time came that the scaffolding had to be removed. As I lay with my precious child in her hospital bed, stroking her hair, touching her velvet skin and singing to her, those perfectly symmetrical walls softly tumbled down around us. They had looked so strong. Like they could bear the weight of a thousand worlds upon them. And they were strong, for a while. But then the weight just got to be too heavy. And they gave way.

And my baby's spirit went to sing with the angels.

"It's beautiful, isn't it?

How it all hurts

but we never

give up."

I found that quote on Kendall's Pinterest page. How true the words. And what a horrible lie. How can I never give up? How can I ever bear this? I know people must because I see them. The parents who have lost children. And they are living. But how? How do I take what is left of myself and force it to go on? The answer for me still is *I don't know*. I truly don't know how to continue to live in a world that should have a beautiful, vibrant, full-of-life girl in it. But I know I must keep going.

"How it all hurts

but we never

give up."

And so, I will not give up--despite the pain. I will trust that I will find my way back to life. To laughter. However long it takes.

But those words. I could not get away from them. People kept saying words to me and I didn't know why. Couldn't they see that my precious child was gone? Couldn't they see my guts spilled all over the floor? Couldn't they see that half of my heart had been ripped out of my body?

But I met their caring eyes. I pretended to hear and understand what they were saying. When necessary I willed my brain to send appropriate words to my mouth in response. Sometimes those words were audible. But most of the time I just didn't see the point.

Outside those four walls it was just another day. People went to work, shopped, played with their dogs, enjoyed the sunshine. But inside those four walls people had been sitting, whispering, praying, crying. Outside was a world away but what I wouldn't have given to be sitting at my desk at work on just another ordinary Monday.

Today, two years later, I'm still fighting my way back from the

Dark Times. That week in the hospital is just one giant blur of sounds, smells, love, numbers, support, unbelievable pain, and kind acts of service. When you've suffered a traumatic, life-changing event you lose yourself for a time. Once we were out of the hospital I felt like I might lose my mind as well.

Ironically, being in the hospital gave me strength. She was fighting so I was fighting. I had something to focus on. A job to do. And being a southern woman and a Mama, I felt I had a responsibility to all the people who were at the hospital waiting with us, like I had to be some kind of hostess, which I resented and appreciated at the same time. I resented it for taking me away from my baby and I appreciated it for the briefest of respites it allowed me. Leaving room 121 to go be with (what I did not yet recognize as) my Village helped create a bit of rhythm to the day, and I looked forward to and dreaded it equally.

But the day did come when I had to walk out of that hospital and leave my child there alone within those four, now crumbled walls. Every fiber of my being was screaming "Don't Leave Her!" but I wasn't strong enough to stand my ground. I submitted to my family's decision about what they thought best.

Brain death is a strange thing. All your senses are telling you your child is still alive. You see her chest rising and falling with each breath, hear the breath entering and leaving her body, touch her still warm, baby soft skin, breathe in her scent, taste the tears on your lips. How could a Mama just walk away from her baby and leave her there alone?! But that is exactly what I did. I walked out of that hospital and into a black hole.

Okay God. Where the bleep bleep are you? I am crying out to you with all I am, all I have. Why are you so bleeping lazy? Why don't you show the bleep up? Here I am!!! WHERE THE BLEEP BLEEP BLEEPING BLEEP ARE YOU?

Grief is a living, breathing animal of prey. It must be fed, no matter the cost, so It takes what It needs when It needs it. And the hunted never know when It will show up to feed. Will you be in the middle of a presentation at work? Checking out at the grocery store? Getting gas? We've seen animals being hunted in the wild. Not one of them just lays down and says "Okay, you win. Let's get this over with." They all run, *fight*, because they instinctively know that it is a matter of life or death. As the hunted, there are days that you have the will to fight and Grief senses that. But Grief has mad skills. It knows your Achilles heel. Knows what buttons to push. Grief has been in and out of your life in different ways for decades, so It bides Its time, stalks you, and waits until your guard is down, then sucker punches you right in the gut. Sometimes It just knocks the wind out of you and you can manage to go on with work-groceries-gas-dry cleaning-yard work and all the other tasks you had planned for that day. Then there are days that It knocks you to your knees and you wonder if you will ever be able to stand alone again. But while you are down there on your knees it does not even cross your mind to pray for strength because eventually, Grief will make you doubt things you had known since you were old enough to know things. You will rail, curse, disavow. Loudly! How could you believe in the loving God you had always known when He *let* this happen? (Grief tells you He *let* it happen, but you know, somewhere at your core, that things just happen. But of course, you are currently blind to this.) Where was He when I was crying out to Him? Why hadn't He shown up at the one and only moment in my half a century of life on this planet when I had needed Him the most for my *literal* survival? I thought those footprints in the sand were His. How could I have been so wrong?

Oh, that Good Laugh I mentioned earlier? To have a good laugh, one needs to be in the light. But at that time and in that space, I was blind to the light because I wasn't ready to see, really see, the love that had been raised around me. The way God *had* shown up and had done many of the things that I had railed, *RAILED!*, against him for not doing.

I was not ready to see that He had met me in the emergency room with someone who not only knew my closest friends but could get in touch with them, that He filled the waiting room with the people who would become the foundation and walls of my Village, the Village that continues, to this day, to provide love and support. That He sent people who would see that my lawn needed mowing, or a dead tree needed removing. And then someone would mow my lawn and remove the dead tree then go on to weed and mulch all the flower beds in my not-small yard! My house was cleaned, laundry done, food was organized and arrived on a regular schedule for weeks. My refrigerator was cleaned out of everything that had become a science experiment then re-stocked. *Who does that?*

All of this took place during a time when I was spending a significant number of my days and nights on the floor in the fetal position, drowning in snot and tears and barely able to tell you my own name. Don't get me wrong, I *"wasam"* angry! (I think I just made up a word to illustrate how difficult it is to let go of those human emotions that want to blame God for death/refugees/poverty/social injustice/fill in your own cause here).

God and I have had some screaming fights. We have broken up a time or two. But in the end, I just could not deny the knowledge at my core that He *is* the Great I Am.

Do you remember the song from The Who called "Who Are You (who, who, who, who)"? Living with Grief is to ask and answer that question for yourself in every contact with every human being, in every situation, every day. Who are you?

I live in a small city. It's pretty much a given that I will see someone I know whenever I venture out. Who will I be in those encounters? The grieving mom? The strong fighter? Part of a benevolent organ donor family? Many times, my "identity" was chosen for me by the person I encountered. I could tell what they expected to see from me by what they said and how they said it. My coping strategy was to go from place to place with my head down, giving myself no chance of having to make eye contact with anyone. On the few occasions that I ate at a restaurant I would insist we sit in a back corner, so I could have my back to the rest of the room, again to avoid eye contact with anyone. And when I did encounter someone who knew what had happened I tried to be all, "yes, what a blessing that she was able to be an organ donor" blah, blah, blah.

But GOD! I was pissed! Why do people get to go on living their lives with my child's parts in them? Why couldn't she keep her parts and go on living her own life having been given that second chance that her organ recipients would have been given? The opportunity to face the enormity of a situation, the possibility of death, and have it change her? The opportunity for her to see brighter colors, for food to taste better, for sunsets to be more beautiful? The randomness of death is something I will struggle with for the rest of my days on this planet. And so, one of my identities became someone who had to show grace to others in extreme circumstances.

I received a thank you letter from a recipient of one of Kendall's organs who said that "God's purpose for 'his' (Kendall's) life" was to give this recipient another chance at his own. Not only did this person not know that my precious child was a girl, he basically told me that God's plan was for her to be born, let her die in a horrible way but not so horrible that she couldn't be an organ donor, then pull his name out of a hat to receive the perfect part he needed to have a second chance at life. Do I really believe that was what he was trying to impart to me? Absolutely not! I think he was trying to help me, using-the-tools-he-had-at-the-time, to find some way to understand her death. He was just lacking in his delivery. (Not to be misunderstood, however, I am and always will be thankful that Kendall had chosen to be an organ donor. It was something we had discussed, and she understood and today I have precious relationships with two of her recipients and have heard from several others. Only 2% of people who die can donate organs and had she not indicated her desire to be a donor, Iwou would have made the decision to donate.)

There is someone I know that to this day whenever we cross paths will give me that sad smile expression and drop her head a bit. I could choose to read this as her only seeing me as the-mom-who-lost-her-daughter, or I could choose to be grateful that she remembered and still wanted to let me know that she did. One of the most important lessons my mom taught me throughout my life was to always try to reframe things that had upset me. I could choose to be hurt or offended by people's reactions to me or I could do my best to meet them with love and choose to find the positive in our interactions.

Time does *not* heal all wounds. Living with Grief is just that, *living* with Grief. Losing a child is not something you "get over". Ever. There is no closure. You just continue to move through it for the rest of your life. It's like trying to swim an Olympic race through mud. You can see all your opponent's moving swiftly through sparkling, clear water but your lane is full of thick, brown mud.

There is no way you can keep up. But you dive in anyway and do-the-best-you-can-do-with-the-tools-you-have-at-the-time   because you know that tomorrow or next week or next month you will be in one of the other lanes with sparkling clear water and there you will swim, lap after lap, until you find yourself in muddy water again.

So where was God when the Dark Times came? He was building a Village right under my feet. Mobilizing troops to meet the needs that I could not even recognize I had. He was tugging at someone's heart to regularly send a card just to let me know my grief was acknowledged and prayers were being said. He was sending someone to literally drive by my house and scrawl "I Love You!" on a scrap piece of paper and leave it on my door - and I will keep it forever because it is that precious to me. He was planting seeds in my own heart that over time would grow into my new "laugh muscles" so that when I was ready I would be able to find my joy again. The Village was built. I was too blind to see it, those hands and feet of God in the world. But like Brigadoon, when the fog lifted, I could finally see it for what it was. God's presence in the Dark Times. There all along. But because the one sacred prayer in my heart and on my lips for five days and nights wasn't answered, I was blind to it. And not until I had spent too many hours to count crying on the closet/family room/bathroom floor, keened, wailed, babbled like a crazy person, attacked my bathroom with a flat iron, the pages of my journal with a pen, and cussed like a sailor was I able to begin to see the faint outlines of the footprints in the sand. And, well, you know how that story goes.

"It's beautiful, isn't it?

How it all hurts

but we never

give up."

I will not give up despite the pain. I trust that I will find my way back to life, joy and laughter. However long it takes.

Proverbs 31:25, "She is clothed with strength and dignity, and she laughs without fear of the future."

Soul Questions

- Reclamation: the process of claiming something back or of reasserting a right. Laughter is a theme in this story. Have you experienced the "bursting forth from the soul" type of laughter described by Carolyn Birmingham? Has there been a time in your life when Herman Mellville's "mighty good laugh" became "rather too scare a good thing"? How did you reclaim your laughter?

- Were you surprised by the author's loss of faith following the death of her daughter? How has your relationship with God been affected (positively or negatively) by major events in your life?

- Do you think that most people intend to outwardly present their most authentic selves? Have you ever found yourself in a position when you allowed others to "dictate" who you were going to be? How did you feel afterwards? Did that experience inform your subsequent interactions with friends and acquaintances? In what way?

You may contact Kimber at kimberspinks@gmail.com and visit her website at www.kimber.soulsinthesand.com

Kimber Spinks

Kimber Spinks was awarded the Most Valuable Player trophy on her middle school soccer team. She's received numerous other accolades as well: Miss Emergency 4 years in a row on her high school drill team, Best Mom Ever for several years running from her precious daughters and Most Likely to Volunteer by her friends and family.

As a high school student in Houston she dreamed of becoming a writer. An avid reader and admitted magazine addict she envisioned herself writing for her favorite genre, shelter mags. Kimber did become a writer of sorts. She wrote term papers as a student at Texas A&M, court reports as an employee of Child Protective Services and final exams as a teacher of history and faith formation. She has written love letters to her children, apology letters (for high school antics) to her mother and composed clever quips for social media posts. But after high school she never again thought of "Writing".

But after a devastating event two years ago she wrote a series of posts on a sharing web site. She has not returned to the site to re-read those posts and really has little memory of the content but the feedback received from those who did read the posts was immediate-- "Write a book!" Kimber would say she is not a writer and that *she*didn't consciously write those posts. Yes, they came from her hand, but it was as if God had taken control and those words just spilled out. Her hand could've been behind a curtain and the words would have found their way to the keyboard. So, is she a "Writer"? You will be the judge of that. But she has a story of love, unbelievable loss, giving and ultimately survival that she wants to share in hopes that what she has experienced might help someone, somewhere find their path as well.

Chapter 9

The Miracle of Every Sunrise: Choosing Joy to Conquer Darkness!

"Joy"

By Lilian Chavira

The majestic colors in a sunrise make a moment at the beach magical and full of peace. How does God paint with His brushes such an artistic mix of colors starting with a black-night canvas? One of the most meaningful moments with the Lord was captured in my soul while waves quietly whispered and I could feel the sand on my wet feet. For those minutes, the world around me shut-down and it was just me and Him, the only one who knew what my heart contained. My deepest pains and my overflowing gratitude all rolled down my cheeks in the form of tears, JOYful tears. How can a 43-year-old woman who grew up by some of the most beautiful turquoise Mexican waters have never looked at a sunrise the way she did on that September morning on the Padre Island, Texas beach? Because I am not a happy careless kid anymore, it took many TOUGH nights for me to fully appreciate the miracle of that breath-taking sunrise.

That morning for the first time after my dad's passing, I could peacefully visualize him smiling through those pastel colored clouds, my spiritual eyes could see again that beautiful and enigmatic smile, a prominent symbol of who he was in this world. Memories of him were rushing fast through my head, from childhood to the very last kiss. Seven months had already passed since my precious old man's death and I had already cried more tears than I could ever count but THIS was different. It was a moment of "letting-go" and recognizing God's mercy on my dad's journey and ours. Before his last breath, life gave him the chance to leave behind everything "fixed" while I was given the opportunity to witness how God could make possible what was on my "impossible list". I could look back to the previous years and what it meant to go through a very deep personal and professional crisis while being mad at a silent God. It is there that I want to start this story. A story of a wife, mom and woman who was trying hard on her own to adapt to the new city and state while playing the role of the daughter of a broken family. This is a collection of the moments that left such an imprint in my soul. A vivid description of why choosing JOY during every circumstance makes a difference not only in the atmosphere and emotions of that moment but on our legacy and on the futures of our loved ones.

So, I invite you to go back with me to the Spring of 2015 when I was desperately praying for the needed courage to jump off the cliff and find "my purpose" again. I was sick and tired of spending the last few years of my life in "survival mode". God was disturbingly quiet while the wrong voices and my own insecurities made me feel so unworthy and out of place. I cowardly built high walls around myself, attending our new town's church on Sundays and caring only for my own little family. I was waking up on Monday anxiously waiting for Friday. Working hard for nothing relevant, getting reports done on-time and hiding behind a desk. Shining a tiny bit had already brought too much pain, so staying "invisible" was the safe way to receive a recurrent paycheck. Where was the unstoppable Lilian and brave entrepreneur that I once knew? I was grieving the loss of her. The dusty memories of that successful marketing professional in the corporate world and courageous woman who had launched her own blooming business were all packed in boxes when we moved from Michigan to Texas in 2013.

However, God did not let that little flame inside me die. Could I find purpose ever again? I was determined to go back to entrepreneurship, but all these business ideas took me to the same place - FEAR. Fear of failing, of making the wrong choice, of disappointing others, of not being good enough. These voices were so loud that I kept to myself all these feelings and crazy thoughts.

Still, with the support of my amazing husband and two awesome teens, I submitted my eight weeks' notice. I did so much research professionally and spiritually during those Summer months, trying to find myself again, that I realized that I could not fix my broken wings. I had to go back to the "ugly crawling caterpillar stage", which meant I should start with a humble heart in a community that I hated for so long. It was imperative to leave the past behind and make room for gratitude. I needed God more than ever so the first step was to get out of my safe haven and selfish mindset. We were blessed by the teaching of our Elevate Life Church, but this mega-church gave me the perfect scenario to embrace my "ghost" outfit. I attended once a week and served once a month, but I had not made any effort to connect with anyone. So, this was the bravest step I could take. I signed up for Fall women's bible study. I picked the address closest to my house, not even reading the title of the book or author. The next morning, I showed up!

I will never forget that day! Beverly Heyberger for me was only a name listed on the website. She opened the front door of her beautiful house where 8-9 other friendly ladies introduced themselves. I cannot even describe the level of anxiety that was hidden behind my smile. Somehow, I went through the social/breakfast part, and it was time to get into the book that I bought on my way there... "The Best Yes" by Lisa Terkeurst. Only a few minutes had passed when I felt like I was alone trapped inside a weird capsule of time. The leader's stunning blue eyes looked into mine with such confidence and beauty. There was love in the tone of her voice and wisdom in every word said. I knew it was God talking to me, only me! Every single word Robin Moore spoke described where I was. My brokenness, anger and vulnerability were confronted by my Heavenly Father in such a tender way. Suddenly,

I could not contain the tears, yes, how embarrassing, right in front of a bunch of strangers! Only because I was a Christian who knew the God I trust, did I not leave that house running in panic, truly thinking that gorgeous blond was a witch and the phone line between God and me had been hacked. It was such a powerful God moment!

I left with red eyes rushing to get home and read more of that intriguing book. What a "coincidence" that the workbook included a diagram to fill out and analyze the different options we could be facing in order to find "Our Best Yes". I got several photocopies and filled them out with all my business ideas. Bingo! I knew which one I would pursue. The idea that sounded the strangest, which for "pride reasons" was right at the bottom of my original list. In the following days, the key elements for this new concept were all flowing while working on our Bible study weekly homework. It was like God was revealing in front of my spiritual eyes the new plan He had for my life. But, was I going to fully trust Him? No, not yet, better to keep it as a secret… what if this crazy idea is too dumb and fails?

During our 3rd morning meeting, while going over the study, seated on a comfortable chair in the corner of Bev's living room, I could hear a quiet whisper in my heart… JOY IN THE BREAKROOM… yes! That would be the name for my new venture, a one-stop-shop with the mission of helping to cultivate a culture of gratitude and honor with employees, customers and partners. Based on my previous professional experience and the outstanding example of my former boss Pat McGrath, I accumulated all these crazy ideas on how to show appreciation, improve engagement, encourage laughter and spreading JOY into the workplace! My new concept would include a full-service specialty catering, with customized gifts and colorful decor for unique and fun corporate celebrations that would creatively bring any company's brand and values to life. Maybe, I could reinvent myself using every talent within me and become a valuable resource for business owners and leaders who had that desire but did not have the time or creative capital to make personal and memorable experiences. Maybe, I could make my own little difference in the corporate world.

I was so excited and with the name in place, I quickly said good-bye to those sweet ladies and rushed out to get home and sketch my new logo. I called two dear and talented friends from Michigan, Romina Davalos my logo designer, and Tamie West my incredible editor. I asked them to be a part of this big secret. I was so anxious, but their loving support and beautiful work ignited my soul. Once they sent me the final jpg and text reviewed I was ready to design the corporate image. No time to go to bed. It was an unforgettable night, out of my home office window, it went from sunset to sunrise while my brochure and business cards were designed. By the time the birds were singing, the prototype for my advertising package was complete and already printed. I was finally dreaming again!

But what does all of this have to do with the sunrise title and the beginning of this chapter? Well, the logo sketched on my homework sheet was the picture of a bright yellow sun shining in the darkness, which was my visible reminder that every day brings another opportunity to become light. If I believed that JOY comes from the inside, a company that possesses JOY internally would shine among others in its industry. Maybe, I could help my clients to somehow accomplish that!

This was such an exciting time in my life that equally paired with the saddest phone calls to my parents. They always loved and supported their children, but during that season, I could not share anything happening with them. They were too busy solving a difficult stage in their lives. After a 42-year marriage, they had been separated for almost ten years. The separation was devastating, and the consequences of selfish decisions were still being paid but somehow, life continued. I had already overcome the discovery of very shocking things about my dad. As hard as it was for a daddy's girl to put together the pieces of a broken hero, I had chosen to honor, love and respect him as the loving and caring father that he always was. But this year, his diabetes was impacting his health and independent living. My mom, out of her kind heart, decided they could live together in a roommate kind of arrangement. He moved to her place. Both wanted to make things work under their own conditions. Little things turned into awful fights, bringing out years and years of unforgivable pains. It was unbelievable, cruel, bloody! What happened with the loving family that raised me to be strong where I learned the value of kindness? The one that used to eat and laugh around the table during Sunday brunches or the most incredible parties? Nothing was left! It did not take long for my parents to hate each other like never before.

Watching my parents fall apart was painful, but deep down, all I wanted was for them to be okay, to not hurt each other anymore. It was very challenging for me as a middle child who lived so far away to become a marriage counselor to my elderly parents. The whole family was involved in such deep and nasty drama. Things went from bad to worse until my dad moved out. By then words could not be taken back and the wounds were deep. I remember ending a call with my mother who was extremely hurt. Have you ever felt like you want to divorce your own parents and family of origin to pretend you are an orphan and single child for the rest of your life? Well, that was me, that day. I hung up the phone promising myself I would never call to listen to that crap ever again... I was done!

During those stressful days when I went back and forth from the excitement of my business planning to constant tears while dealing with my parents' drama, I had to go to my annual check-up and things did not look right. I was sent for a biopsy. This would be the sixth one in my history, so I knew what was coming. Although the anxiety of "waiting" is always nerve racking, it was a moment of hope when results came back okay. However, because of my previous findings and family history, doctors wanted to schedule a surgery and remove a sizeable fast-growing tumor to explore what was around it. The phantom of breast cancer was back again. I could be the next one to receive that diagnosis. By then I was scared, so scared! Coming back from the hospital with my husband out of town, I remember feeling this deep internal darkness. That thing called JOY that I was thinking of spreading through a business idea suddenly seemed unreachable in my personal space. I went to bed devastated!

But here came the sun again and God's new mercies! Somehow, I woke up with a clear decision. Although my feelings did not align with it, I knew I needed to open a door to forgiveness. All I could control was what I would allow to grow in my own heart. Maybe, just maybe I could choose JOY. It was then or never. I called my husband asking him to get a plane ticket to go to Mexico City for a weekend. Before the scheduled surgery, I needed to see my parents and siblings to remove this heavy load that I was carrying. As always, my amazing man supported me, stayed with the kids between his business trips while I flew early Friday morning. My family was broken in two, so the plan was to spend the first 36 hours with my daddy and some of the grandkids. The next 36 hours would be with my mom, older brother and the other part of the gang who were on her side after the big fight. Me and my beautiful younger sister had become closer than ever and we were determined to enjoy this time, love them both and have fun together. I wanted so bad to forget the harsh words once said trying to replace them with memories of these magical days. It worked! That was one of the most AMAZING trips ever. We toured the city in a convertible car with a fancy Italian dinner and hotel night with my daddy. Next, we enjoyed the most delicious home meals and went to a fun karaoke place and sang our hearts out with my mamma. We laughed, hugged and took many pictures in both "scenarios". A family divided into two parts was our reality. However, for me, it was undeniable: hate makes you sick, forgiveness heals your body, JOY lifts-up your soul and God… God will always give you one more sunrise that comes with the chance to conquer darkness. One more day to live to the fullest!

I flew back ready to have that scary procedure on December 18th, 2015. Though I was frightened when entering the hospital, there was peace in my soul. Peace between me and all of those who I loved. My faith was stronger than ever. Because of God's mercy, the surgery was a success and the results came back clean. Without deserving it, life and health were given back to me. It was my choice what to do with them. I quickly recovered during the holidays and I remember thinking on New Year's Eve, from the day I decided to insert the word JOY into my business name, God allowed circumstances around me to teach me the real meaning of it (even though I had been labeled by others as a positive and happy person). This was different, it was a new sunrise with all the "colors" of life encountering each other, and that was the enigmatic beauty of it.

It was January 2016 a brand-new year! As soon as my kids went back to school I grabbed all the drafts designed during the previous seasons Bible study and I finished a complete business plan. Time to work for that dream! Going door to door and introducing my new business concept to complete strangers was the hardest thing I have ever done. Building a concept from the ground up (or below ground) was exhausting, frustrating, humbling and yet so rewarding. The journey has been tough, but I have never been alone. Even with the many struggles, my business is growing. Day after day, God has been placing the right people at the right time, amazing human beings that today I am honored not only to list as my clients, I can call them FRIENDS. They are FAMILY! Earthly angels and miracles exist and keep showing-up after numerous discouraging nights.

However, during that very challenging beginning, months and months of extensive work and the financial stress of money going out but no orders coming in, it was a blessing to have my mom, dad and siblings fully on board supporting me long distance. Family was

still messy, but they were happy with my new journey. Especially my daddy, he was always the best "dream listener". He did not interrupt you or instruct you, he listened! Once you asked for an opinion, his voice, full of passion, gave you the best advice ever. He loved that my new concept was going to have so much to do with food, art and people. Those were all the loves of his life. Hospitality was his career. He was an icon in his industry nationwide, highly recognized for his leadership skills, art, and incredible creativity represented in the most luxurious and impressive buffets he and his teams created while managing resorts and owning restaurants in Mexico. I could tell during our calls he was so proud of me, always encouraging me to never give up. "You will see the light at the end of the tunnel", he said. Many would call my concept "cute" but nobody was hiring me until one day a beautiful couple, well-known locally as The McMortgages booked my first "Employee Monthly Appreciation Ice Cream Bar". That was such a needed breakthrough. I called my dad immediately and I heard the excitement in his loving voice… but at that time, his health had started to deteriorate quickly.

SafePro Pest Control was next establishing an employee appreciation plan. Finally, I could see a ray of sunshine! Weeks later, one friend I met at the Bible study who knew the story of my entrepreneurial journey recommended me to her publisher. I was contacted by UImpact with the invite to co-author the book "Behind Your Brand". What? Me? How? My parents needed to hear this! I will never forget my father's reaction, he was blown-away and for the first time, he did not let me finish and said: DO IT! YOU CAN DO IT! I think I said "YES" to that scary project because of his incredible support and unexpected reaction.

As days went by, we witnessed how dementia was impacting my dad's daily life, our conversations were never the same. My brilliant little sister insisted that we should improvise a trip in October to celebrate both of my parents' birthdays. Since I was going home, to see me, they had to compromise. They did! After that horrible second separation mom and dad were present in the same place blowing their birthday candles (seated on two different sides of the table). My dad acted strange most of the time, but he greatly enjoyed all the restaurants we toured. Food was his passion and to see him eating was a pleasure. I said good bye with the idea of returning to Mexico in December to spend Christmas together as a family for very first time in 12 years. My mom agreed with the plan and my dad smiled saying "I'll wait for you my love"!

The holidays were approaching, and my business was slowly growing while my dad's health got worse. My sister and nephews were taking such good care of him, but it devastated me to be so far away. A door I had been knocking opened and I got to design two holiday parties for the city of Frisco employees. Wow, so rewarding! I also managed to focus, write and submit my chapter for the book "Behind Her Brand". As soon as I finished, I headed to Mexico with my husband and kids for the holidays. My mom also traveled to meet us there. My daddy was so sick by then. For Christmas we joyfully cooked the turkey and our traditional dishes, but when I tried to feed him, he started screaming asking me to take it out of his mouth. My soul shattered and that was the moment I knew his last days were close. Somehow, God gave me the strength to keep the energy up. I got the Santa, Mrs. Claus and elf hats out and we took many fun family photos. What a treasure for generations to come. I only had to say, "Daddy smile for the picture", and he did. The next second his mind would drift away again. God allowed us to make many precious Christmas memories together. What a blessing!

However, during those days my mom avoided being close to my dad. He was upstairs while she was downstairs, or they were on opposite sides of the sofa. The next afternoon I had to go out with my kids for a quick visit. My sister suggested to my mom to go upstairs and give my dad some company while she was going to take a nap. My mom went, and my dad reacted to her presence. Miraculously, his mind suddenly "came back" for three incredible hours. He talked to my mom and for the very first time in his entire life, he asked for forgiveness and told her all the things she needed to hear. Those words healed some of the most profound wounds he had placed in her heart. They held hands and did something never typical in their marriage, they

prayed together! Pride was finally left aside. He invited Jesus into his heart asking God to wait for him in heaven.

When we arrived, we could not believe what happened, something like that was in "my impossible" file. Oh, the healing and forgiveness both offered and received during these miraculous three hours! It is incredible what forgiveness does. We were all around them, listening to our favorite music and singing together, bringing memories back and laughing. My dad kept telling stories of the beautiful 16-year-old girl who stole his heart. She was the love of his life, he said. My mom held his hand with so much love and tenderness. She repeated to him the same words. When he started to feel tired, he closed his eyes, and his mind was gone again. It was the most amazing miracle I had ever witnessed. It was magical, so incredibly precious! The next days were sad taking care of him knowing it was time to go back home, my kids needed to start school and my husband his traveling. My father for a few minutes was aware that I was leaving, he kissed me saying, "Te amo munequita linda". "Love you my pretty baby doll", it was the last time he pronounced those words!

As soon as I was back in Frisco, for the first time I was hired by Haiman Hogue Law Firm to cater breakfast at the Frisco Chamber of Commerce. My heart was breaking with my dad's updates but at the same time I was so honored to be following in his footprints. I kept thinking of his professionalism and that gave me strength. The breakfast buffet was a huge success and right there I was asked by Kevin Hodes, another member to design a second one in a couple of weeks. Finally, the clients and opportunities that I had been praying for so long were here! Right when I was loading the car with the display for the next design, my sister called. Dad had a stroke and was rushed to the emergency room. I started looking for my client's phone number to apologize, he would understand, right? But I realized this could close those doors at the chamber forever. Then I asked myself, what would my old man do in my shoes? The answer was simple... I was going to finish my commitment, wait for my husband to fly back home to stay with the kids and then leave. I could not sleep at all that night, I set up breakfast early the next morning. Everything turned out gorgeous and I managed to keep that big smile on my face, the same smile I always saw on my dad when hosting events. The support and love received by members and friends there was unbelievable. I could not ignore the presence of JOY in that room and every sweet text received along this nightmare. After I finished the event, I was flying to Mexico, I could hardly catch my own breath!

I got to the hospital after dad's brain surgery. Looking at him with all those tubes was the most painful scene. His condition was critical. During the following days miracles of forgiveness continued to happen. God made the impossible, possible! Although the relationship between my oldest brother and my dad had been damaged for years, my sweet big bro came, bringing with him tender love and strength for us. He took care of my dad every night and I am sure something radical happened between them in that hospital room. My two older half-sisters were also a sweet presence. My aunts and other relatives were loving on my daddy as well. In the middle of so much pain, there was so much love! The memories of those days with my dad are gold. His body did not respond but I know he was listening to every single word. Tears in his eyes were the sign. As a family, we have now so many hospital stories that will live with us forever. During this tragedy, hope, love and JOY were fully present.

I was going back and forth to Mexico, with the launch of my "Behind Your Brand" Book approaching. The publisher knew my difficult situation emailed me wondering if I would attend. But God and my dad had already discussed that topic. I am certain they had conspired together to make sure I would not miss the book launch and that he was going to be present, watching and smiling from heaven. The timing was so incredible, the pain so indescribable but the JOY was so real. I was able to attend the launch party the morning of February 6th, a day after I flew back from my dad's funeral. How could the timing be so precise?

That day, I wanted to stay home, the pain was unbearable but instead, I dressed up and put a smile on my face. My tribe would be there! My rock and loving husband, bible study leaders, mentors, clients and some of my incredible friends! Robin Moore, Anita Stokey, Tamara Burkhart, Lori McCaghren, Maria Martinez, Ann Burt, Stephanie Lyons, Claudia Chavez, Sheila Williamson, and Konni Spitzer held me tight, so I could be strong. A favorite quote of mine became once again real that morning. "When life gives you a hundred reasons to break down, show life that you have a million reasons to smile". That day, I grabbed the microphone to talk about a business that I founded with the mission of spreading joy. And joy is supposed to come from the inside, never depending on the circumstances. Joy is fueled with gratitude. At that moment I felt devastated but also exponentially thankful! That day, I met Lisa Pulliam another co-author and compiler of this book that you are reading now. It was a divine connection that would take me months later to the "Toes in The Sand Women's Retreat" where I witnessed that incredible sunrise in Padre Island. A time by the ocean where deep in my soul I admitted that God was the God of the impossible. The One who is working during every circumstance and ends up connecting all dots. I could see then how choosing JOY overcame my deepest darkness. God performed miracles during the last days of my dad's life. He restored an unfixable family. He helped me to find my new purpose in life. His beautiful touch was evident every morning in my husband and children's lives, our resilient marriage or my blooming business. Most important, I was amazed by how the Heavenly Father had never failed that 18-year-old girl who grew up in church but did not believe in unconditional love, marriage or

Christianity. The one who challenged Him one night saying: "If you are real, fill this painful emptiness in my soul and I will let you write the rest of the chapters in my story". Jesus Christ came into that girl's heart and her life changed FOREVER. A new day arose, hope was found, and a new legacy started only because my story became HIS!

"Weeping may endure for the night, but JOY comes in the morning" Psalm 30:5

Soul Questions:

- What about you? What is your impossible? Have you given God the pen to write your story?

- Can you recognize at least one miracle in your life that came after your darkest night?

- Instead of staying in my bed after my dad's funeral, regardless of how I felt, I chose to go to the book launch where I met Lisa. How are you going to choose JOY in your current circumstances to give room to miracles?

Contact Information:

Email: lilianchavira.soulsinthesand@mail.com

Websites:

lilianchavira.soulsinthesand.com

joyinthebreakroom.com

Lilian Chavira

Lilian Chavira is an award-winning entrepreneur, published author, founder of two companies but mostly, she is a passionate dreamer and a woman of faith! Originally from Mexico, she met the love of her life during college and they married three years later in El Paso, TX. She earned a Bachelor degree in Business while working in Marketing & Design.

In 2004 her husband was transferred to Okemos, MI where they raised their children Daniel and Sarai. Her children were the inspiration for Lilian to start her first business venture, a gourmet bakery "Petite Pleasures by Gellocake" that was later featured in USA Today, as well as 19 statewide, local publications and TV shows. She was recognized as the 2009 Meridian Emerging Entrepreneur of the Year by The MARC/MISBTDC in Meridian Township. Four years into her successful venture, Lilian and her husband were faced with a difficult decision: a promotion offer for her husband in Texas that they believed was a great next step in his career. Although Lilian was deeply sad to lock the doors on her booming business, she knew in her core that her family was her first priority. Lilian found herself encouraging her amazing husband to accept this promotion that would relocate them to Frisco, TX.

Relocating a family with teenage children is never easy. Yet as Lilian remained strong on the outside for her husband and children, she felt her own entrepreneurial goals and dreams slipping away. Never had she thought she would let "life" pull her down to the point that she could not remember the un-stoppable woman she was once. After a very dark season, a cancer-scare and surgery, she gave God her broken pieces and found in Him the courage to reinvent herself again. She began to understand new meaning for the words "joy" or "success" and being led by PURPOSE. Now, as founder of "Joy In The Breakroom" Lilian wakes up every morning determined to let God shine in her despite her own flaws or surrounding circumstances. She is passionately taking "gratitude" to a new level in the corporate world while treasuring her family, committed to make a difference by leaving a legacy and humbly recognizing her mission of building-up every woman around her. She fights daily for JOY and is now a part of a MASTER PLAN much bigger than herself.

Chapter 10

Be * You * † * Full

Beautiful

By Sheri Martin

My arms felt heavy, outstretched as far as they could reach to opposing sides of the bedroom. The soft texture of the floor embraced my full body; tears streamed down my cheeks, flowing. My body laid helpless as the sounds from my gut surfaced and released into the air, like that of a crying infant. Visions drifted inward to unimaginable screams where my voice could not be heard. I cried out to God in hopes of hearing His answer. This morning's prayer was going to be different. It was time for me to forgive and let God take over.

My story really begins years earlier. It was a Thursday evening in August 2015. I was preparing to host a fun girls' night out event out in my home, and the hostess was due to arrive at any moment. As I was getting ready, I noticed my husband had a guilty expression on his face, and was withdrawn. I had seen this same look many years earlier; I sensed something was wrong yet had no clue what it could be. I began to ask what was bothering him. In a single, quick snap of a finger, my life was forever changed. I remember hearing the words, "Sheri, I am not physically attracted to you". It was as if time stood still, and everything that happened next was in slow motion. I stood in shock, staring, and in disbelief. How could this be happening to me, again? These same words were spoken about ten years earlier. They keep resurfacing. The power of words can change a person. Positive words come and go, but one negative word sticks with you forever. I was brought back to reality by the sound of the doorbell. As I opened the door and greeted the Sales Consultant, my first words to her were in the form of a question, "Are you a Christian?" With a puzzled look, she answered, "Yes. I am". I quickly asked if she would pray with me and explained that we needed to cancel the party. We did both. I believe God places people in your life at the right moment, and this moment is true as well. She was my angel that night. I am forever thankful for her presence.

I believe, wholeheartedly, in the sacred covenant and my wedding vows that I made before God on January 19, 1991. How did things go so wrong? How did I go through the motions of living under the same roof, in two separate rooms, without speaking? I felt the aching, raw emotions that a person cannot express verbally, the kind you feel deep in your bones. I felt nauseous. Simple tasks became daunting, and I found it harder to stay focused. Food was not appealing to me in the least, and I began to lose weight. I was eating about 400 calories per day. Internally, I was sad, lonely, lost, unloved, and felt unattractive. Surprisingly, I would run across friends, and they would tell me how great I looked.

I found this quite ironic. At night, my new normal was to stay awake until my body gave out from complete exhaustion, sometimes until wee hours of the morning. I attempted to live my "normal" life by going to work daily and being a mom to my daughter, who was 16 at the time. Our son was already out of the house, serving his four-year commitment in the United States Air Force. Every new day felt the same, like I was living in a fog. I took longer baths because I could hide and cry longer without my daughter seeing. I wept often. My whole body would shake uncontrollably all the time. Feeling nervous was a constant. I tried to remain busy and stay active with my running. However, having no appetite made running extremely difficult, especially for my longer runs. One day, I was about four-miles into an eight-mile run, and I had to stop and walk. Crying made it impossible to breathe. I finished the other four-miles, walking and sobbing. I realized, rather quickly, that I couldn't do things I loved anymore because I wasn't eating. Every October, I ran in a local ten-mile race, and in 2015, I finished. The night before, I slept only two hours and almost talked myself out of showing up for the race. Something inside of me said, "Do not let anyone steal my joy." I cried most of the course. I finished that race feeling like I had my personal record best; of all my marathons and half marathons, this race I am most proud of completing. I will always cherish my friends for dropping their own plans to come and support me! My running friends became like family, and their encouragement during my trial helped keep me sane. It gave me something to do most days instead of feeling sorry for myself.

"If you change nothing, everything remains the same." This is an anonymous quote I remember reading. We made changes. In 2017, we sold our large dream house and downsized, as empty nesters, into a new townhouse. I believe any house can be made into a home. It's all about the finishing touches and the personal touch you bring to a property to make it a home. I believe in adding sentimental items into a space that adds special meaning. I love to decorate, and I poured myself into making our new place special. Normal became normal again. Fast. Each day seemed like a scene from the movie Groundhog Day, the same as the day before. I began to really understand how excluded I was feeling, and once again, felt insignificant. I felt like a roommate; I felt lonely living with another person. One night while sitting on the couch, quietly, solemn, I glanced over and noticed that I was not alone in the room, yet never felt lonelier. This was a big epiphany moment for me.

The easiness to tears was like turning on a faucet. Most days were like a roller coaster, free falling with my hands up, screaming. I found it most difficult to concentrate on one task at a time; simple jobs took longer than they should have. I felt like I was living in a horrible dream. "Sheri, I am not physically attracted to you," became my daily record player. I added more negative words to them, "I am not pretty enough", "I am not skinny enough", "I am unloved" etcetera, fed my mind. I knew this was not helpful, but I kept listening to the auto repeat button. I am a very outgoing person, the type that never meets a stranger. More irony. Around feeling beautiful, I was now insecure. Sadness was my new friend, my constant companion, dwelling in my soul. I hid this well. The Bible does not say we will not encounter trials. It says we will all experience setbacks. I thought I had already gone through my biggest struggle; however, God had a different plan in store for my life. Psalm 34: 17-18, "The righteous cry out, and the Lord hears them; He delivers them from all their troubles. The Lord is close to the brokenhearted and saves those who are crushed in spirit." This verse helped me get through a lot of days. My heart was broken. I did not understand why it felt like someone I loved died. I prayed to God daily, never questioning Him, I certainly doubted my circumstances. I never gave up Hope knowing God had better things in store for me. I talked with many friends, my Pastor, my children, my parents, and they all prayed for me as I went through the motions of life, feeling lifeless. My Dad called me every day. My son called me at night. Everyone was concerned, deeply. I could not comprehend letting God down with my covenant, I tried everything to make things better.

How did I end up alone at age fifty? This is not what I wanted at all; however, I would rather be alone, than lonely. This was my big epiphany God showed me that night on the couch. It was time to stop looking in the rear-view mirror and start looking in the windshield at the wonderful view ahead of me. This always reminds me of the story in the Bible about Lot's wife in Genesis 19:26, "But Lot's wife looked back, and she became a pillar of salt." I think there is a lesson there for us today. Do not bring up negative issues from your past; instead, look at the possibilities ahead, even if you are unsure what they are. Trust in God. God Says in *Jeremiah 29:11, "God's plan for your life is to prosper you, not to harm you".* I may not have known what God was planning for me but stayed confident knowing He was in charge. This is what keeps me moving forward. One day, my decision was to take a leap of faith. I LEAPED…hired movers, packed my car, turned up my car dancing tunes, and began my new journey forward. I moved to a new town, knowing only one person locally, leaving 35 years of memories, friends, church, clients, and even my book of business behind. I trusted God's word and put it to the test in my own life. I would write down verses, pray without ceasing, and read my Bible. The Bible is a source to help equip us with the tools we need to fight our battles, I have many verses that are in my toolbox to use whenever necessary. If you are reading my story, my prayer for you is to find the verse(s) that speak to you and add them to your own toolbox. I had the faith as a mustard seed, *Matthew 17:20, "Truly I tell you, if you have faith as small as a mustard seed, you can say to this mountain, 'Move from here to there,' and it will move. Nothing will be impossible for you."* A journey for my new beginning and a better Sheri was in motion. I remember pulling out of Houston, creating a goodbye video, and feeling the complete spectrum of sadness and excitement at the same time. I do not think I am extraordinary. I feel like God lives within me, and His light shines through me. Moving into my new one-bedroom apartment took all my remaining energy. It proved to be quite an overwhelming day for me. In addition to moving and saying goodbyes, I had to unload my car, go up three flights of stairs with every trip, and unpack each box. I was beyond fatigued. That was my first indicator of what living alone was all about. No one came to help me unload. With my focus remaining forward, I once again, created a small apartment full of Sheri's flare. This was my new home.

In *Matthew 18:21-22, Peter asks Jesus, how many times should we forgive someone who sins against us? Jesus replies "77 times".* We are all sinners, yet we are called to forgive and show grace to those who do wrong against us. Forgiveness is for our own sake and the beginning of the healing process. I knew the importance of forgiveness from past life experiences. I started to feel differently. I felt angry, mad at what had happened to me and my children. I noticed the left side of my upper lip would curl up and cause a physical, negative scowl. I felt like the Grinch. Thinking about my current circumstances hit a "boiling point" internally, like a cancer taking over my soul. How did a positive person become so bitter? This was not who I was, nor who I wanted to be. I had to make a change. I know that good and evil cannot co-exist in the same body, yet it felt like there was a battle inside of me. One had to get out, and it was time for the EVIL to go! That was my crying out prayer that certain morning with my arms outstretched! I cried out to God to help me forgive. I asked God to let me move ahead without resentment and feeling like the victim. I prayed to help me meet a man that would be my yoke, someone that was my equal, in every way. That morning after my gut-wrenching prayer of asking to help me show forgiveness, I felt a release of anger. The curl in my lip was gone. I started being more positive and living life again. I chose joy again!

It's surprising to see my story unfold both with the joys and sorrows that transpired. Those first three months in my new town were very dark days and prompted my anguishing prayer. I have never felt more alone and relied more on God than any other time in my life. I was working and tried to be productive. Outwardly, it appeared my life was "fine". I joined many different networking groups, volunteered with my favorite charity, and slowly visited a few different churches. I began going through the motions of living, and eventually even started to date!

My life changed completely when I met a man with my silly sense of humor. He brought a smile into my heart that had been gone for far too long, and people noticed my giddiness. I feel like God brought this wonderful man into my life to show me that good things do happen from bad situations. One of my favorite verses is,

Romans 8:28, *"And we know that in all things God works for the good of those who love him, who have been called according to his purpose"*. My prayer was answered. I thank God for my many blessings, my family, new and old friends, and for bringing happiness back into my life.

Psalm 136, "Give thanks to the Lord, for he is good for his steadfast love endures forever". I believed this even when I was unsure about what was happening, I knew God had a plan for Sheri. As I write these painful words, they still 'sting'. However, they do not have ownership anymore, nor do they define who I am. A friend of mine gave me a special Bible verse that I prayed more than any other: *Psalm 139:14, "I Praise you, O Lord, for I am fearfully and wonderfully made. Wonderful are your works; my soul knows it very well"*. God showed me through my struggle to rely on Him, and that I do not need a man to validate my beauty. I am beautiful. God created me in the exact image He wanted. The old saying, "Beauty is as beauty does" rings true. I had to learn to love myself for who I am. My inner beauty shines! I have a great passion for the Lord and want to share that with others. I am a strong capable woman, who is creative, funny, intelligent, giving, loving, caring, and *beautiful*.

I do know that my situation is not unique. Sadly, lots of people have similar stories of loss, but I never knew those individuals. This story is mine. All mine. The emotions I endured were gut-wrenching, but somehow, with God as my leader, I came out on top. I pray that my testimony helps other women know they are not alone and encourages them to seek guidance in their own lives. Reflecting on my horrible, amazing journey brings me to one word. **Beautiful**.

The word *beautiful*. I decided to break it down into different sections and share what I learned from God. **BE*YOU* +* FULL.**

BE:

The first section of the word beautiful is **BE**. God wants us to **Be** still and listen to His voice. Psalm 46:10, *"**Be** still, and know that I am God; I will be exalted among the nations, I will be exalted in the earth."*. Louie Giglio said it best in his book, "I am not, but I know I am". He talks about the word BE is the same as God, so, when we read **Be**loved, according to Louie Giglio means LOVED by God. I know without a question of a doubt that God loves me, Sheri. He loves you too. He created me in the womb. *Psalm 139:13, "For you created my inmost being; you knit me together in my mother's womb"*. I am His vessel. Psalm 100:3, *"Know that the Lord, he is God! It is he who made us, and we are his; we are his people, and the sheep of his pasture"*.

I've finally learned how to be comfortable within my own skin. My belief is that exercise is key to a healthy lifestyle. Running is my niche. So "I run straight to the goal with purpose in every step" 1Corinthians 9:26. However, learning about kickboxing has allowed me to let out some anger on the bag, plus I get cardio workout. I had to just **BE** and be happy with me. Our body is God's temple and we should take care of it. *1 Corinthians 6:19, "Do you not know that your bodies are temples of the Holy Spirit, who is in you, whom you have received from God? You are not your own"*.

YOU:

The Michael Jackson song "Man in The mirror" has always been a favorite. If you listen carefully to the lyrics, they are powerful. I have taken a deep look into the mirror, searched my soul, and listened to God for answers. I have prayed more than ever before, crying out for Him. I have seen things I do not like about myself and have worked on improving certain areas. My personal goal is to keep striving to be a better person and using my gifts to help others. My feelings are that "most" people do not look at the real issues (or the mirror). They try to fix problems with material things. That is the easy way out. It takes a great deal of courage to be aware of what you need to do to improve yourself. Courage builds strength. Nothing about this is easy. The first step is taking that look and admitting areas that you want to make a change. There is power behind momentum or moving forward. Simply take steps in the direction you want to go.

+ CROSS:

If God brings you to it, God will bring you through it. This is true with anything. I learned to lean in, trust God more, even more than I already did. I thought it was a good idea to move to a new town, where I had one friend. That is crazy at age 50! Starting my real estate business over completely and living on a fixed budget was a huge challenge. I often cried in my new one-bedroom apartment. I was tough on the outside. Despite that, the tears would come as soon as I unlocked my apartment door each day. Throughout my whole struggle, I always made my bed, kept my home clean, and remained positive. A lot can be learned from a person by looking at how they live. If you live in chaos, there is a high chance your life is in disorder. Making a bed seems like a silly detail. Nonetheless, it gave me a routine and made me smile when I returned from work to a clean, well-kept apartment. Hebrews 11:1, "Now faith is confident in what we hope for and assurance about what we do not see". I could not see the future yet had the faith. My CROSS could also stand for CROSSroads. Keep the faith on your own journey.

Full:

God provides and wants us to have abundance. My cup runneth over. Help others find a local charity to give back. One of the first things I did when I moved was to locate a charity that I believed in. I always had a place in my heart for Habitat for Humanity, so I signed up and became a volunteer. I ended up painting the exterior trim of the whole house, once they found out I knew how to "cut in". I know the importance of helping others also takes the focus off oneself. To much is given, much is expected. *Luke 12:48, "But the one who does not know and does things deserving punishment will be beaten with few blows. From everyone who has been given much, much will be demanded; and from the one who has been entrusted with much, much more will be asked".*

Beautiful is a combination of different aspects plus the joy of inner self. May God bless you on your own journey and keep you in the light.

Romans 8:28

"And we know that in all things God works for the good of those who love him, who have been called according to his purpose" NIV

Soul Questions:

- What are three qualities about your body that you feel are beautiful?

- What life lesson would you want to pass down about relationships?

- Write a short story/vision about your life in the future, include goals, details, and why you would want to succeed to reach the goals in your story. Look forward through your windshield.

Sheri would love to know how her story impacted your life. You may contact her at SheriRealtor@mail.com or find her on social media!

Sheri Martin

Sheri Martin is a Realtor® in the Dallas/Fort Worth Area. Sheri believes that integrity is more than just a word and lives with this as one of her main core life values.

In her spare time, she enjoys exercising which includes running and kickboxing; She has completed two full marathons and numerous half marathons, and uses her time running to talk and listen to God. Sheri enjoys being outdoors and lives a healthy lifestyle, yet, still likes chips and salsa on the weekends!

Sheri has a passion for God and lets others to see His light shine through her. Her smile is infectious, and she never meets a stranger. Fun is another one of Sheri's core values. She believes that being engaged in life is part of the journey, and one should find joy in the little things. One way she finds joy is by volunteering for Habitat for Humanity; she believes by helping others we learn more about what truly matters.

Sheri is a dedicated mom of two wonderful kids. Her son served four years in the United States Air Force and now lives in Colorado. Her daughter shares in her mother's artistic skills. Both children play the guitar, trumpet, and keyboard; they feel music is a daily part of their lives.

Before launching her real estate career, Sheri taught Art and Photography in the public school system for 14 years. One of her favorite quotes "I alone cannot change the world, but I can cast a stone across the waters to create many ripples"~ Mother Teresa. Sheri is an Artist and actively paints and take photographs; she is a positive, creative person who expresses herself through her artwork. She sees herself as God's paintbrush.

Chapter 11

The Treasure Chest of Legacy

"Revealed"

By Lisa White

Treasure #1: Shocking, unexpected circumstances in your life do not thwart God's plans for you.

We had celebrated a magical winter! Our first beautiful child Rebecca was born in late November and as a result, Thanksgiving and Christmas were filled with laughter, delight, and promise. Hearts were full. Every day was like an invitation into a brand-new life with our baby girl. After an extended maternity leave, in February I returned to my job at Garland High School where I taught English and coordinated a program for gifted students. I had been back at work for a couple of weeks, pounding out my new normal, when the shrill sound of the phone jolted me from my work. The receptionist told me I needed to call my babysitter's house right away. (What? Did she say, "right away?") A fog crept silently into the room, and I had trouble dialing the number. It was 2:40 pm on a Wednesday, and the sitter's friend choked out the words… my twelve-week-old daughter had stopped breathing and was in the emergency room at a local hospital. A friend drove me there. After sitting in the chaplain's office for what seemed like an eternity, word finally came on her condition. The nurse told me a respirator was breathing for her, and the medical team had been trying for ten minutes to get her heart to start beating again. My husband had not yet arrived, and all I could do was cry out to God, repeatedly, for Him to let her heart – please – just start beating again. The doctor was reluctantly preparing to come out and tell us there was nothing more he could do, and then her heart beat twice. God answered my prayer. He gave us a miraculous three more days with Rebecca: three days in which she was in a coma, and three days in which we could learn to say goodbye.

After the medical team got her stabilized, she was transported to Children's Medical Center in Dallas. After multiple assessments and a full medical team briefing, it was revealed she had a one percent chance of survival. In angst and shock, my heart asked how it could be possible for a healthy 3-month-old to suddenly have her life hanging between heaven and earth. Yet the angst and shock joined together with soaring crescendos of faith that with God, all things are possible – even the one percent chance of survival. Agony and ecstasy hung on every measure. Between tests, scans, consultations, and a million rhythmic machines pumping temporary life into our daughter, we were buoyed up by the presence of family, friends, and colleagues from work. During those three days, the Polaroid camera in my mind's eye can still recall the snapshots of Rebecca's legacy: so many people at my workplace now wondering about faith and seeing it in action; our Young Married group from church showing up by the dozens bringing warm muffins, strength and love; all the parents who went home in the evenings and hugged their own children a little tighter. Sometimes fifty or sixty people would be gathered in the waiting room with us, hearts collectively hoping that somehow our daughter would survive. On that Friday, tests revealed that her brain stem was not responding, and we needed to consider our options. Her very wise doctor suggested that after having slept on the hard floor for two long nights, we should go home, sleep in our own bed, think it over, and come back the next day to let her know our decision – whether to take her off life support. It was Valentine's Day.

That Friday night assured that Rebecca's grandpa and her nurse would be up all-night taking care of her, we went downstairs to the valet station where we had left our keys two days and a lifetime ago. The driver, making small talk, asked us if we were visiting someone at the hospital. We explained that our daughter had been there since Wednesday in a coma and this was our first time to leave. He immediately looked at us, and in hushed tones he slowly asked, "Are you Rebecca White's parents?" My incredulous response was a question: "Do you know who she is?" He said, "Everyone here knows who she is." Agony and ecstasy now had a new companion: parental pride and an increasing sense that this situation was much, much bigger than what our eyes could see. God appeared to be multiplying His influence on countless people through our daughter by adding those three days to her life.

At home, we discussed the doctor's conversation with us earlier that day. I had one burning question on my mind: if we took Rebecca off life support, would we be interfering with that one percent chance for her to live? I had believed God was bigger than statistics, and that He could restore her life and health. The difference now, though, was that instead of her medical team deciding, WE were being asked to decide – with huge ramifications and crushing weight. The doorbell rang twice that night, each time revealing one of our dear associate pastors from the church, each time offering strength, wisdom, and prayer. Their visits were comforting, but my question remained. I decided to call Heather, the nurse who was caring for Rebecca that night. After a reassuring update that our baby was doing fine after a diaper change and some music, Heather asked me how things were going. I explained my dilemma; that I didn't know if we were interfering with God's plan if we took her off life support. Heather replied, "Well…I'm no expert, but I've always believed that if God wanted someone to live, then they would live, even if they were taken off life support."

Wow. Peace coursed through my heart – the weight of the world lifted off. It wasn't up to us whether Rebecca lived or died, it was up to God. God knows how to make a way where there seems to be no way, and the same God who parted the Red Sea could not be limited by two young parents deciding whether to take their daughter off life support. We could leave the outcome in His hands knowing that He sees the big picture and chooses what's best for us even when we cannot understand. So, we made plans to dress up the next morning and embrace the likely event that she would be leaving this earthly home and taking a trip to her heavenly home. We had been present when she entered this world, and we were to be present if it was her time to leave this world. It was a solemn occasion.

The next morning, we gave the doctor our decision to remove life support. The doctor explained that they would cap all the tubes and wires and turn off the beeps, so we could hold our baby girl during her final minutes. A quietness settled on the room that had been our world for three days. As the curtain was drawn, and it was just the three of us, we told her it was alright for her to go to Jesus; He was that bright Light in front of her. He would take care of her. We told her we loved her, and we would see her again. She stayed with us about half an hour then slipped off into Paradise.

Sudden Infant Death Syndrome, or SIDS, occurs in babies who are usually one to six months of age, and no one knows the cause. At that time the medical community had found no signs which show one baby is more likely than another to die from SIDS. Neither my husband, nor I, nor the sitter could have done anything to cause this, or to prevent it from happening.

After signing paperwork to donate her vessels and valves, we went to the funeral home to pick out a coffin. Spending time with family and planning the visitation and the funeral filled the following days. Each decision kept us focused and connected to Rebecca. These were precious moments, once in a lifetime moment – we realized her funeral would take the place of one day seeing her graduate, one day walking her down the aisle, one day holding her first baby. Her whole future which we had already envisioned was boiled down to this one event, and afterward all we would have were memories. Her funeral, attended by hundreds and hundreds of people, was perfect and difficult, celebrating her life, and celebrating a Savior who made a Way for us to see her again in heaven.

Then came the hard part. I had been strong for her during those most difficult days of her life, but she was gone now, and it was time to mourn. I cried as I sorted through all those precious little clothes, holding them to my nose to smell her one last time. I cried as I took her Johnny Jump Up off the door frame, remembering her dancing as I played the piano for her. I poured some of my grief into writing a song about my Baby Angel. One day I realized I didn't have my car – the last time I had driven was two weeks earlier on that day when time stopped; a friend had stored it for me. Everything reminded me of our life with her, which was no longer to be. The grief was unimaginable.

During that time, I recalled a couple of events that became treasures to tuck away in my heart. That last Wednesday of her life, during the entire 45-minute drive from our Dallas home to Garland, she had stared intently at me, rear-facing from the front passenger seat. At the time I was so puzzled – she STARED at me for 45 minutes. Since I now knew that was the final car ride of her life, I'd like to think she was filling up those big blue eyes with her mother's face, loving me with her gaze, perhaps knowing it would be the last time she would see me in this life. Another unlikely love notes occurred in that Garland emergency room the first time we could go in and see her. I can remember feeling terrified as we walked through those big double doors, not knowing what we would find on the other side and feeling even less unsure about what to say and how to act. As we approached the white sheets cradling our daughter's motionless body, tubes and beeps everywhere, a decision surged through my heart and out into my actions. I needed to be strong for her and for her dad, so I wrapped those tiny fingers around my index finger and talked to her. I told her how brave she was, and that mommy and daddy were right there with her. I told her we loved her and were so proud of her. What happened next seems impossible from a medical perspective – she squeezed my finger with her little hand! Her brain had been deprived of oxygen for so long and just could not survive that kind of trauma. But somehow those fingers gave me one last good bye to treasure for the rest of my life.

God's grace beamed through the darkness: in all those Polaroid snapshots; in the surprising words of the valet driver; in her gaze on the last car ride of her life; in the squeeze of her fingers. Hebrews 1:3 says, "The Son is the radiance of God's glory and the exact representation of his being, sustaining all things by his powerful word." I love that! His radiance transcended my circumstances, and He did sustain me by his powerful word. In our little duplex home, when she would be going to sleep or playing in her room, I would play a lullaby tape with soft, calliope-like melodies and words straight from Scripture. My favorite song, which was sung at her funeral, began like this: *"By the Lord, for the Lord, you were created. You were created to bring him honor and praise. Tiny hands, gentle eyes, fingers and nose – every part, set apart, to bring him glory."* *(See Revelation 4:11)*

Five weeks later, we spoke on a Sunday morning in front of the congregation of our church, and my recorded words still echo the shock and surprising awe of that week – filled with the depths of facing one of a parent's worst nightmares, and the elation of the Savior's very presence, more real than the rhythmic sound of the respirator.

"One thing that God has taught us through this, is that He can take our flawed, human attempts to live our daily lives, and He can add His magnificent power to do His work here on this earth. Before this happened, I would have imagined that this pain would have been awful enough to cripple my outlook on life, and to bring me to a dysfunctional halt. However, God can surround us with His awesome peace and love – to the point where we can claim victory over death because we know we'll see her again! It may be 50 years or longer…it may be tomorrow…but however long we are separated from Rebecca, eternity is longer."

Next was the really hard work of going on with life without my daughter. A couple of months after the funeral, my friend Mary Grace invited me over to see the nursery she had decorated in anticipation of her little bundle soon to arrive. As we reveled in the beautiful designs, she finally explained, "Lisa, I'm supposed to tell you something. I don't understand the message, but all I know is I'm supposed to tell you. God said you are getting ready to go into a desert, but not to worry because you will come out on the other side." I had never heard anyone give me a message from God like that, so I paid attention, but I didn't understand what it meant. I thanked her and tucked it away in my memory.

Treasure #2: You are not responsible for figuring out your legacy. You are only responsible for seeking God in the present moment.

My journey into the desert began soon enough. It started with more unexpected situations in the same year of Rebecca's death: my parents' divorce; the shooting deaths of two friends; the relocation of my sister and her family to Houston; and the relocation of my husband and myself to Tyler. Grief and survival and careers put a strain on our relationship, exacerbated by our inability to conceive. For three years we were parents with empty arms. In 1994 we were finally blessed with a beautiful son! Then exactly one year later, our second beautiful son was four-days-old! Aching arms were finally full. The greatest joy of my life today remains getting to be the mother of my two incredible sons. They are amazing, and their adult lives, just beginning, are full of promise.

Back in the desert, careers were calling, and our relationship was derailing. Life was hard and demanding. That first Mother's Day, in May of 1992, my mother-in-law had given me a pink bible with devotions for women built right into the pages. For that first year, I drank in every devotion and devoured God's Word as if my life depended on it. Walking out that first year was unbearable without the oxygen of God's revelation through His Word. But as time wore on, depression started to settle into my heart. I got busy trying to make a life rather than looking to Him for Life. The full crescendo of faith had faded, and a shadow of hopelessness began to fall. In my attempt to get ahold of my life, I settled my focus on my little family. I didn't understand it at the time, but I now know I had two subconscious goals during that period: to make sure my sons didn't die, and to make sure my family had everything they needed to be happy. Neither was in my control.

During my time in the desert, I had one constant question continuously languishing in the deepest part of my soul. Why? Why did she have to die? Why did our hopes and dreams have to be dashed? Why did we have to continue in a life with this heartache? I didn't blame God. I just didn't understand why things had to be this way. I knew that thousands of mothers throughout history had been through the deaths of their children, and I knew somehow, they had survived, gone on to live their lives, and had been in the grave many years now. In the big picture, I knew life would go on, but I didn't see how to get there from the desert. I kept putting one foot in front of the other. My life seemed to be spiraling downward. I felt incapable of accomplishing my two goals, and I felt completely ineffectual for God.

During that time, I worked at a public high school in Tyler. I was the coordinator of an international program for motivated students. Many of my students would hang out in my office between classes, during lunch, and after school, and often they would ask to be my student aides during a free period in their schedules. I enjoyed hearing about their lives, encouraging them in their studies, and helping them think through their challenges. One such student, Abbey, was smart and capable and did well in her classes. She didn't open up easily, but I could tell she was searching. By this time, I had moved my pink bible, the one my mother-in-law had given me on my first Mother's Day, to my office in the high school. When presented with difficult questions, I would look through my pink bible to find answers. Even though my life was feeling increasingly hopeless, I still knew in my mind that there was no substitute for Truth – anything less is hollow and unfulfilling. Plus – to be completely honest – I didn't like to be wrong! If I could find the answer in the bible, it seemed more likely to be right even in the case of user error!

Through her time in high school, Abbey would present different questions to me about life. They were always veiled. I didn't know the whole story, but I also sensed it wasn't wise to probe into areas she wasn't discussing. When the time came for her to graduate, she had extenuating circumstances and was to be moving out on her own. Realizing my limits but still wanting to help her launch well, I bought Abbey a pink bible. I took time to underline passages that were meaningful to me, and to write notes to her about topics she had brought up in our conversations. Life continued, and I didn't hear from Abbey again for a long time.

About thirteen years after she graduated, Abbey contacted me through social media. It wasn't just a polite reconnection for old times' sake. She wanted to know what I remembered about the time she was in high school. She was going through a process of rediscovering some repressed memories and was questioning the circumstances of her youth. What she revealed to me was shocking. I had no idea. She was doing the hard work of sorting through her life in counseling, and part of her therapy was to contact certain people she had trusted when she was younger. As the conversation continued, she told me a story. After graduation, her life had taken a downward turn. She had looked for worth, security, and relief from her pain in every path available to mankind. One day she was going through some boxes and found the pink bible I had given her years earlier. She began reading that bible, and she started discovering a Truth around which she could build her life. She started learning more about God. And she eventually began a relationship with Him, accepting Jesus' gift of salvation. She went on to become a therapist, working with abused children. Her life's work, filled with strong faith and influence to help people become free from their shackles, could have begun in any way God chose – and He chose to use me (among others) and that pink bible, inspired out of the death of my daughter, a gift that brought healing to me and went on to help bring healing to Abbey. But here is the very interesting part. For more than twenty years, I viewed that desert time of my life as a time of failure, hopelessness, and utter worthlessness for the cause of Christ's kingdom. I did not even recall giving Abbey the pink bible. God uses our lives for His purposes despite how we feel about our usefulness. Our legacy is not up to us. Legacy begins and ends in the heart of God. We are only called to seek Him in the present moment and say YES. How freeing to know that our lives matter even when our feelings falter.

Treasure #3: God is constantly revealing hidden treasure that He wants you to find.

Another important treasure came out of the desert. When I was at my lowest point, the realization came that I needed to take active, intentional steps to move out of my hopelessness. I knew in my head that God's plan did not include hopelessness. What then was standing in my way? It was fear. Fear of the consequences of rocking the dysfunctional boat that had become my security. Fear of being rejected. Fear of the unknown. I weighed both options on the scale – keeping things the same or making those difficult changes – and realized by keeping things the same, I was losing myself. By making changes, there was no way to go but up.

One of the intentional changes was to again read God's Word in earnest. I would read large passages at a time, asking God to give me insight. One day, sitting at my kitchen table early in the morning, I came across a passage in *Isaiah 43: "Forget the former things; do not dwell on the past. See, I am doing a new thing! Now it springs up; do you not perceive it? I am making a way in the desert, and streams in the wasteland."*

Immediately God revealed that He was speaking very personally to me through those words. I remembered what my friend Mary Grace had said to me previously, in the weeks after Rebecca died – that according to God, I would go through the desert but not to worry, because I would come out on the other side. Could God be calling me out of the desert? I asked Him and waited expectantly for His answer. A few days later, I was standing by my kitchen sink. The old familiar "why" question had come to mind. Suddenly, I knew God was speaking in my soul. He saw my heart. He knew about my desire to know why. He loved me with absolutely no condemnation.

He revealed to me that the answer to my why questions would not come in the form I was seeking. Instead, the answer was His Son, Jesus Christ.

His Son. Jesus Christ. I didn't understand, but a shower of

peace washed over me that day, and I was never plagued by the why questions again. God has revealed countless treasures to me over the years since He pulled me out of the desert. He has revealed promises to me at times when I desperately needed them, and through His timing He has revealed Himself as well.

Deuteronomy 29:29 says, *"The hidden things belong to the Lord, but the things that are revealed belong to us and our children."* How many times have we looked so intently for the hidden things, and thought it unfair of God to hide them, when instead we could have been enjoying the many things He is revealing, and claiming them as our own?

Treasure #4: The life you are building will be tested with fire, and what remains after the fire is your legacy.

One day everything you and I have ever done will be laid out in front of us and a match will be thrown on top. Only the things that are eternal will remain, and the rest will burn up, no matter how good we thought they were. 1 Corinthians 3:12-14 says, *"If anyone builds on this foundation using gold, silver, costly stones, wood, hay, or straw, their work will be shown for what it is, because the Day will bring it to light. It will be revealed with fire, and the fire will test the quality of each person's work. If what has been built survives, the builder will receive a reward."*

Our legacy is what will remain after the fire. Shocking, unexpected circumstances in your life will not thwart God's plans for you. You are not responsible for figuring out your legacy; you are only responsible for seeking God in each present moment. God is constantly revealing hidden treasure that He wants you to find. The things that are revealed belong to you. Legacy begins and ends in the heart of God.

2 Timothy 1:9-10 ~ *"He has saved us and called us to a holy life—not because of anything we have done but because of his own purpose and grace. This grace was given us in Christ Jesus before the beginning of time, but it has now been revealed through the appearing of our Savior, Christ Jesus, who has destroyed death and has brought life and immortality to light through the gospel."*

Soul Questions

- What are some ways your life has turned out differently from what you expected or planned?

- What is one thing God has revealed about Himself to you through nature, through a friend, through a situation, or through His Word?

- It has been said that fear is faith in the enemy. What fear is holding you back from trusting God? Can you hand that fear over to God and let Him set you free?

To connect with Lisa White, visit her website:
www.LisaWhite.SoulsInTheSand.com.

Lisa White

A native Texan, Lisa White grew up in Dallas, Texas, earned her B.S. in Education from Baylor University, and taught in public schools for 18 years. During that time she married and gave birth to two inspiring sons, Preston, and Philip, now grown, and one daughter, Rebecca, who lives in heaven. Lisa's career in education was followed by a career in employee benefits as a licensed Life and Health Insurance Agent, then a brief career as an Epic-certified Instructional Designer, all in the beautiful Piney Woods of East Texas. She currently serves as a Corporate Client Engagement Coordinator with The Flippen Group, a Texas-based LLC that provides strategies and services to help individuals, schools and companies thrive.

Through a series of losses that threatened to cripple her life, Lisa has learned that God specializes in creating beauty from ashes, that His promises are true, and that He is faithful. His redeeming work in her life has led Lisa to serve as Women's Minister in a Tyler church, and to disciple dozens of women by pouring out God's grace through her life. Lisa is an avid student of God's Word, of learning new ways to apply it to real life, of fervent prayer, and of empowering women to understand their legacy in Christ.

Chapter 12

Sea Glass in the Sand

"Blessed"

By Tracy Tidwell

Close your eyes and imagine being on a beach somewhere, listening to the sights and sounds of God's great creation of the ocean. You listen to the waves, slowly moving your toes to feel the soft sand under your feet. Your hair blows with the wind. You couldn't be happier, more peaceful and closer to our Lord than right in this moment. You open your eyes and look down at the sand and there in the sand, you spy a piece of glass. Sea glass! You reach down to pick it up and, in your hand; you can feel the soft round edges and can closely examine the beautiful frosted look of this sea glass. As you gaze at this beautiful piece of glass, you are reminded that this piece of glass took between 30 to 40 years to become what it is in your hand. At one time, this was a broken shard of glass, tossed into the ocean through circumstance. And now, through time, its edges have become smooth, and its brilliance reflects years of being tossed around in waves of activity.

This is my life. I am that piece of sea glass, tossed around over years through life and its' experiences and circumstances. The one and only reason it's beautiful is because of my Lord, Jesus Christ. The one and only reason that I am beautiful is because of Him. I am blessed and highly favored and deeply loved by God. *Deuteronomy 28*

I was born in church. I was raised in a Southern Baptist home. I prayed to ask Jesus to be my Savior when I was six. My dad was a school principal and my mom was a stay at home mom. My dad also served as a deacon in our church. I am an only child. Yes, my mom and dad sought perfection and got it in their first child. Ha! My best friends growing up were my church friends. I was a very sheltered young lady. I was taught manners, respect and the love of Jesus. My parents believed in the scripture "spare the rod, spoil the child" and applied that to me more times that I care to share, but

I knew right from wrong and I had a respect/fear for my mom and my dad. When I started driving and would go somewhere with friends or dates, my dad always said, "don't ever do anything that would hurt our last name". Meaning, I better behave or else. In my household, I was expected to make good grades. So, I did. I graduated with honors as an honor grad. In my household, I was expected to go to college, so I did, with scholarships. However, we never had alcohol in our house. I believe this is where my glass was first tossed in the sand/water originally. I joined a sorority in college and truly don't remember much about my first two years in college. I joke now and say "jungle juice was my college frenemy" but, I was my own worst enemy. I truly didn't know how to handle life itself and being in college and basically on my own for the first time, I started making my own decisions and many of them were not great. And that's all I have to say about that. I woke up in places that I couldn't even remember going to the night before. I lost my scholarship, moved back home and transferred colleges. I am still amazed that I graduated with my first degree in four years looking back at all the poor decisions I made. But remember, I am blessed and highly favored. God totally protected me from so many things that could have been much worse.

While I was in college I met an amazing man who I will always be grateful for. He was sweet, kind and we fell in love. I think. I hope that makes sense. I don't know if at that point in my life I knew what love was. My mom and dad had some tough times in their marriage, but when they figured things out in their relationship, they had the best relationship I think I've ever seen in a married couple. They loved each other and when my mom found out she had stage 4 Renal Cell Carcinoma, my dad stayed by her side. When we placed her in hospice care, he was with her 23 out of 24 hours a day, going home only to shower and change. That's love and dedication. So, I have seen true love. Love is a choice we make every day. We must make that choice with our significant other each day because some days may not be the greatest. But in college, love was a "feeling" and the time was right. All my friends were getting married so when this man asked me to marry him, I of course said yes based on a "feeling". We had three beautiful children together, Andrew, Nicholas and Katelyn. And because of these three beautiful God serving children, I now have four grandchildren and one on the way and two beautiful daughters in laws. I've heard people say, "I wouldn't change a thing about my marriage because my kids came out of it". Well, I would change a thing or two. Or three. Or four. I would've changed my attitude and changed the type of person that I was. And I would've changed my walk with the Lord and how I treated my husband. Oh wait, let me be specific, God would've changed me to be more Christ like if I had asked Him, but I didn't ask.

You see, I wanted to have it all at that time. I wanted the perfect life with the Barbie and Ken look. Perfect children, a great house, nice cars, good jobs, etc. It was all about what was on the outside and not what was on the inside that counted for me. After fourteen years of being married, I realized I wanted out. When we got a divorce, everyone told me they never saw that one coming and that we looked like a perfect family. And that's the way I wanted it. Yes, I raised my children in a Christian home, but to truly teach them what their purpose was here on earth I didn't get quite right. I thought I even deserved better than what I had! How selfish of me. But that was the old self and my old self had plenty to learn. My shard of glass again was tossed about in the ocean to and fro. I didn't understand back then how blessed and highly favored I was. All I knew was I wanted more. More passion, more fun and a greater lifestyle was what I was looking for and had not experienced with my husband. Not more of God, but more for me. It was all about me. When my divorce became final, reality set in. I had to learn to live the lifestyle of a single woman raising my children. And that's when God really begin to show me the things I needed to change. As I progressed in life as a single mom, things weren't as easy or as fun as I thought they were going to be. I had bills to pay and children to teach what was right. And throw dating into the mix; well let's just say it wasn't what I thought it was going to be.

As I prayed daily and asked God for wisdom and tried to listen to Him at every turn, He began to mold me to learn how to be a *Proverbs 31* woman. God began to show me what a real wife should look like from the inside. He began to show me that I needed to change from the inside. He shared with me that I was worth more than I ever thought I was. I was worthy and didn't even realize it, but it was Jesus who made me worthy. You see, I learned that I was worth more than the money in my bank account. I learned that I was worth more than the price tags on my clothes. I learned that I was worth more than my level of education. I was worth more than the number of friends I had. I was worth more than my accomplishments in life. I was worth more to Him than many sparrows as it claims in *Matthew 10:29-31*. It took me a while to get this, but for those of you reading, I want you to understand that Jesus wants you to know that you are also worthy and blessed. Satan tries to tell us lies about ourselves. He thrives on our insecurities. But Jesus says that we are worthy and blessed. During this time, He was changing me and changing my heart, I knew at that point that I had changed the way I thought about myself, my life, my children's lives and other lives around me. I knew God was showing me how to be a great Christian woman, a great Christian mother and a great Christian wife the next time around.

Now, I wish I could tell you that because of what the Lord has shown me, I was a great Christian wife today, but I can't. I have been through other relationships in my life and haven't found that *Proverbs 31* man either. I wish I could tell you that everything I've learned has been applied, but it hasn't. In fact, negative people and situations have occurred in my life where I've cried out to God "what the heck just happened?" Have you ever cried out to Him with those words?

My sea glass has suffered through dreams shattered, commitments unfulfilled, and hearts broken. I was married two more times and even engaged to another who married someone just a few months after we broke up and I realized that he was seeing her or talking to her while we were engaged. I have a business partner that calls these situations "noise" in life and tells me to tune it out and keep focusing on the goal! Sometimes I've been the cause of my own situations and sometimes Satan has worked through people in my path. Satan knows just what will get my goat too. Glass shards again tossed about in the ocean. But I know this. Wherever I may stumble and fall, God's got me in His Hands. He will never leave me or forsake me. I know what I need to do daily to let my light shine to others, no matter what my situation or circumstances may be. So many people are looking for their "purpose" in life. Billions of dollars have been made from others trying to sell their view on what my purpose is. But the Bible tells us exactly what our purpose is. *Matthew 28:19* states *"Therefore go and make disciples of all nations, baptizing them in the name of the Father and of the Son and of the Holy Spirit".* Now, you know as a Christian your purpose, so no more buying self-help books related to your purpose! You're welcome!

My life has been full of shenanigans. And by that, I mean that God has placed some interesting people and things in my life. Some good, some not so good. If you followed me around for a week you would totally understand. I love adventure. I love to travel. I just love fun. But while Jesus wants us to be joyful while we are on this earth, this life is not about us. I was an educator for 27 years and I've heard excuses after excuses from children, parents and teachers. I should write a book about that but that will be for another time. Schools have some very interesting things happen inside their walls. Some will make you die laughing and others will make you break down into tears. Some things can even make you want to pull your hair out and wonder why in the heck you are in education. God had another plan for my life though besides retiring from education. He gave me my own businesses to run.

Currently, I run two very successful businesses and I'm a music minister at my church. I told you my life is full of shenanigans. I never wanted to become an educator. My dad was a principal and I had seen enough of school activities to last a lifetime. However, when it came down to it, my first degree ended up being what I had enough hours to graduate with and that was in education. It seemed like a good solid choice while I pursued other degrees, of which I did later. However, God just knows what our fortes are, right? Along with a gift of gab or, as I like to put it, communication, I also learned that He had given me a gift to speak and teach. Why are we amazed when God puts us right where we can best be used? I've been blessed to be able to do a lot of international mission work through my churches over time and isn't it amazing that wherever I go, schools just jump out at me and I end up training teachers there too. So therefore, it came as no surprised when God got me out of the schoolhouse and into owning my own businesses as an entrepreneur and, you guessed it, educating people daily on how to live differently. I remember as a classroom teacher I would pray that God would place a full-time overseas ministry in my path so that I could "let my light shine" in tons of areas abroad. I truly wanted to go live in Africa and be a missionary there teaching teachers and students and helping to build things there. One day when I was selfishly praying and frustrated over why God hadn't opened those doors to MY plans, He spoke to me. And I quote, *"Tracy, why would I send you overseas to do something that you should be doing daily in the position I have you in right now"*? Whoa, God! Mic Drop! He is so right. If I wasn't sharing about the love of Jesus Christ where I was, then why in the world would He send me to another country? I had to learn to live in His Will daily, being on the lookout for people to tell about Him and to help. I had spent so much time on what Tracy wanted that what He wanted was forgotten and ignored. I was so tired by the end of most school days that if I had to run into the grocery store to pick up something after work and saw someone I knew, I would turn and go the opposite direction to avoid them. What a change now when I see someone I know in a store and I smile and say "hello" and strike up a friendly conversation. Even if it means just a hug or a word of encouragement, to that one person, it may mean the world. All my life I have felt unworthy of the things that I have received in my life. I wasn't ever good enough or skinny enough or enough to be worthy. But God wants us to boldly know that we have been made flawless through HIM. He created us in His image. He made me flawless, worthy and blessed and He made you in that same fashion as well.

We are so blessed and yet, we don't look for those blessings in everything that we do. My prayer daily is not *"God please bless me if you feel like it"* but that prayer is *"God, thank you so much for the blessings that I know you are going to bestow on me-abundance of blessings and help me to not miss one single blessing!"* I used to think that God had blessings for everyone but me. He had miracles in store for everyone but me. When my mom wasn't cured of cancer at age 65, I yelled at God a few times. Why heal so many and not my mom? Why was my beautiful third grandson born with Down Syndrome? Why wasn't I the one who could've been married for 50+ years to the man of my dreams? The whys just kept on adding up. Until I realized that it was me who was mourning in self-pity and self-absorption. God had a plan A for my life. I messed up plan A, plan B and a few other plans (I'm probably on plan M or N somewhere) yet, even with stupid mistakes and regrets in my life He still picks me up, dusts me off and puts me right back where I should've been all along. I've always been a "fixer". I want to "help" God fix things just in case He can't do it on His own. My prayer many times was *"God, please help me today"* and then I'd go and do what I wanted and try to "help" God get things done in my life. God doesn't need my help. He can do it Himself! Imagine that! And all I must do is be obedient. Wow imagine how much simpler my life would've been if I had been obedient all along. Again, those shards of glass being tossed around in the ocean. Darn glass! I hate to admit it, but I still have days where I am not obedient. I am still a work in progress, but I am worthy and blessed.

As a single woman, I want to share with you that you can be strong. You can stand on your own two feet and you can be successful at anything that you do. We don't need a husband or a significant other to be who God wants us to be. I see so many women struggling with this. They think they must have a boyfriend/husband/significant other to claim their identity. Stop thinking this way. If you rely on Him, He will be ENOUGH. Yes, it gets lonely. Pray harder. Yes, it gets frustrating to do everything myself. Listen longer. We are missing out on so much that our Lord has to bless us with because we think we are defined by who we are with. He provides all our needs. And that does mean ALL! And get ready, because Satan knows your insecurities, so he will put people in your path to try to steal your joy. Claim Psalm 37:4-7, *"Take delight in the Lord and He will give you your heart's desires. Commit your way to the Lord. Trust in Him and He will act, making your righteousness shine like the dawn, your justice like the noon day. Be silent before the Lord and WAIT expectantly for Him. Do not be agitated by one who prospers in his way by the man who cries out evil plans."* You see, we can never be good enough on our own. He sent His Son to shed His blood so that we could live with Him for eternity if we choose. We have been made flawless through His Son and we are worthy and blessed through Jesus Christ. We can never "work" ourselves into Heaven by doing good works. He has allowed us free will to choose Him. We must be dependent on Him. If you feel you are in a battle right now, we must put on our armor of God daily. Whatever you are wearing today, ask Him to bless it as your battlefield armor. I'm telling you, there is a battle going on today and we must be prepared for it! Satan wants you. But God wants you even more. Consider how precious your soul is when both God and Satan want it. My friends, Jesus rescues. When you struggle, He rescues. When you awake, He rescues. When you go to sleep He watches over you. No need for dependency on anything but Him.

That ugly broken shard of glass that was picked up and tossed about in the waters, over time, becomes beautiful. You are beautiful. I am beautiful. Jesus has molded us into this beautiful piece of frosted sea glass. No matter where you have been in life or what you have been through in life, we are overcomers, changed over time and through situations to become beautiful smooth pieces of sea glass. Every wrong turn I've made has made me trust Him even more. Broken glass made beautiful by the Lord. My children now are productive members of society and serving the Lord in their lives and I have so many friends that have been brought into my life who desperately need to know that they are blessed and worthy. And on those days that I may not be feeling blessed and worthy, I can look at a beautiful piece of sea glass I have that was given to me by a very dear friend and remember that all the things I've gone through in life have made me blessed and worthy. I am that ugly shard of glass that has been made into something beautiful and new. He has prosperous plans for you and me. Don't miss out on everything that He provides daily for us. Seek Him with all your heart!

Remember that blessed hymn "How Great Thou Art"? It was written as a poem by Carl Boberg back in 1885. Carl was walking home when church bells began to ring and out of the blue, a thunderstorm began. He hurried home and as he went into his house, he opened a window and looked outside. The storm had calmed, and a rainbow had appeared. He wrote these words:

O Lord my God! When I in awesome wonder
Consider all the works Thy hand hath made.
I see the stars; I hear the rolling thunder,

Thy power throughout the universe displayed.
Then sings my soul, my Savior God, to Thee:
How great Thou art, how great Thou art!
Then sings my soul, my Savior God, to Thee:
How great Thou art, how great Thou art!

We serve a great God who knows you are worthy and blesses you daily. Be looking for those blessings in abundance.

Jeremiah 29:11-13

11 For I know the plans I have for you," declares the LORD, "plans to prosper you and not to harm you, plans to give you hope and a future.

12 Then you will call on me and come and pray to me, and I will listen to you.

13 You will seek me and find me when you seek me with all your heart.

Soul Questions

- Prayerfully consider your blessings in your life. What are the blessings that you realize and what are the blessings that you may not view as blessings now, but claim them as blessings for a later date?

- What are some things that make you feel unworthy in your life, whether it's circumstances or people?

- Do you just talk about walking by faith or really depend on Him to walk by faith? Write down one time where you had complete dependency on Him. How did that time make you feel?

You may contact Tracy at

TracyTidwell80@gmail.com

281 467 2577

Tracy Tidwell

Tracy has lived in Crosby, Texas for the past 33 years but originally is from Sulphur, Louisiana so she is truly a Cajun at heart! She has been an educator all of her adult life. She is a proud single mother of five children and four wonderful grandchildren with another one on the way. She enjoys using her God-given gift of music to sing and play piano and is passionate about serving as worship minister at her church. After years of enjoying a career in education, Tracy saw an open door of opportunity in the world of direct sales. As she stepped into entrepreneurship, she began to see new possibilities for her life. She had always worked hard and lived paycheck to paycheck but being in business for herself allowed her to discover a new path to financial independence. Her life motto is "We are not promised tomorrow so live as if every day is your last".

There's an old saying "You don't know what you don't know". That was Tracy before she launched into her own business. Now, Tracy puts her teaching skills to use in a different way, educating people on how to lift themselves out of the daily rat race of working to pay bills and truly change their financial situation while living a life of purpose and impact. Tracy believes that God blesses us when we are obedient to His path. And Tracy feels blessed beyond measure that He places people in her life daily whose lives she can impact for the better.

Chapter 13

The Sun Will Shine Again

"Resilience"

By Courtney Dowdy

It was over. I had failed again. I lay on the carpet in what used to be our bedroom, sobbing uncontrollably, feeling worthless, wondering how things could have gone so wrong. What was I going to do? I was committed to my marriage and I wanted my family to be whole. I wanted my kids to have the family life I didn't have, I wanted stability. I pleaded out loud, "God have mercy! Have mercy on me, have mercy on our children, have mercy on my family." We had been through so much together. We were broke and broken and had three children. I knew that he was hurting, and there was nothing I could do to ease his pain. I replayed the last 24 hours and then the last 12 years of my life over and over in my head. Devastated, I lay in total darkness beating myself up for the actions of another and questioning whether I had played a role in this. What I needed more than anything right now was someone to hold me. I needed love, and I hated myself for being needy. Today was supposed to have been the first new day of making our dreams come true.

A few months before, we had made the decision to move out of our house and into the family RV park, so my husband could manage and maintain it. Not long after this decision, a new job opportunity presented itself to him. My husband and his friend were certain the job was a sure thing. It was going to be our big financial break, so the plan changed. Now, I would resign my position as the Assistant to the Principal and manage the family business instead. With just a few weeks until school was set to start, I walked heavy-hearted into my school, and gave my verbal notice with tears streaming down my face. I felt like I was letting down my boss and all the parents and students that I loved and had become invested in. I hated this plan; quitting is not something that I do, and I was breaking a signed employment contract, on top of it all. I was angry that once again I was having to sacrifice what I wanted. Every few months it seemed to be a new plan. A friend of mine once asked me if I ever asked him for a "map to his world". A map that changes every day is not a map after all but a selfish, misdirected, non-committed plan that lacks focus. However, I knew I needed to be "on board" with "the plan" or he would resent me for standing in his way.

He and his friend picked me up from work that afternoon to go "celebrate". We started with martinis at a local restaurant bar where I was informed that we were not ordering food. "Tonight, we are on a liquid diet" the friend said. Then, more martinis downtown. Finally, back to the RV park where they proceeded to drink and talk and talk and talk. I remember going out to the friend's truck to get my purse. The silence was deafening there. I could feel the heaviness of the day fall upon me. I closed my eyes and I dozed off in the front seat. The next thing I knew, we were driving down the hill. I am not sure when the friend noticed me in the truck. I remember saying I would just walk back up the hill. He reached over to what I thought was the handle to open my door, but instead, he started kissing me and a second later my door flew open with my husband yelling. A fist fight between the two ensued while I went running back up the hill.

After he came back up the hill to our RV, my husband pulled a rifle from the back bedroom. I was staring down the barrel of a .22, terrified as he walked down the short hallway toward me. I felt fear encompassing me and my face burned hot. I could barely hear myself screaming "I am so sorry, I was not trying to kiss him". I heard the words "I'm sorry" ringing in my head…but they seemed lost in the commotion. The father of my children, gun in hand, yelled, "I'm not going to shoot you!" As I pleaded with him, he pushed me aside and told me to leave, ordering me to get out of his place. He headed back out down the hill with me screaming after him, praying he wouldn't murder his "friend".

I do not remember getting into my car and driving back into town to the house. The storm was raging out of control in my life and in his. With the sudden death of his father, a miscarriage, and the death of my parents all within a few years' time, we found ourselves in deep, emotional turmoil compounded by our individual grief, loss, and financial stresses. In that moment I had no one. I felt I deserved no one and I had nowhere to go. Several years before, we had had a brutal argument that resulted in him punching me in the face. I fled to my mother's house and took refuge in her arms. But my mother was dead now. She had passed away a few years before from breast cancer, and I thought I could handle no more sadness or heartache. How could she have left me when I still needed her?

And now, I lay, sobbing alone on the crappy carpet of the bedroom floor that was once ours. I lay there feeling used, a feeling that was all too familiar. I could feel anger building inside me, bubbling like a volcano. I found my anger fueled by his hurt, and what he perceived as my betrayal. WHY ME GOD? What more must happen in my life? I worked so hard in counseling trying to work through my past. My first therapist had even called me the "comeback kid", saying I was like one of those inflatable boxing toys that gets punched but pops right back up. I wasn't so sure I could keep popping back up. I felt myself falling deeper into a hole of self-loathing, and I replayed in my head a lifetime of abuse, desperately searching for answers and trying to find a reason why. The cards were stacked against me. All the work in therapy was gone; everything I had rebuilt in myself crumbled to bits that night. Memories of being molested as a child flooded back into my mind. Thoughts of my early 20's being date-raped by some jerk who was supposed to have been a friend. Hand over my mouth, in my late 20's, being raped at a beloved family vacation spot in the very next room where my husband and children slept. I couldn't physically call out, and if I were able, would one of my girls hear me first? Oh, how I could not let that happen. MY GOD, when would it be enough? I could not breathe. There is a moment during trauma where your mind separates from your reality. I used to think it was that our emotional being just shuts down. In retrospect, I feel it is where God, His angels, and His protectiveness *must* step in. PLEASE GOD, step in! I asked the Lord to reveal to me the purpose of all this pain and hurt. What was he trying to prepare me for? Surely, he was preparing me for something better. At some point, I fell asleep, right there on the floor. Nothing would ever be the same. And though I had not initiated any of this pain, I felt responsible.

There was a short time of reconciling after I filed for divorce. He promised counseling and agreed to try. But one day that summer, we put the girls on a bus in Dallas for camp, came home, and he calmly told me with a duffle bag in hand that he wasn't happy, and he was leaving. He took the family dog, and like a sad country song, I knew he wasn't coming back; it was over. I was still mourning the death of my mother, my best friend, but the divorce sent me spiraling out of control. To dull the pain, I turned to alcohol, in addition to the antidepressants I was already taking. Issues with my children added to my grief and hardships. One of my daughters was in therapy and was diagnosed with a "mood disorder". Our oldest daughter, a teenager at the time, spent time at my house and then at dad's house depending on who would give her more space or freedom. My youngest struggled in school as he spent a week with dad and a week with me. As a single mother, I could barely pay the bills. My saving grace was my ex-husband's mother who allowed us to stay in the house that she owned. She continued to support me by helping immensely with my children and giving me the tough love that I needed. I can never thank her enough for being the strong woman she was for me in those times. I didn't have to pay money to live there; but the strings attached, were like a noose around my neck. My ex-husband frequently reminded me that I was a *guest* in *his* mother's house. I couldn't keep up with the housework and laundry. I began believing the words of my ex, that I was a terrible mother. I was drowning in debt and *stuff*: My stuff, my mother's stuff, my kids' stuff, my ex's stuff. Depression was a ghost who frequently overtook me.

A few core friends helped me keep afloat. Thanks be to God for my friends. They came to my rescue and my defense many times. They, too, gave me doses of tough love. Most of all, they reminded me of my beauty, my grace through Christ, and my worth. I continued trying to find my focus, going through the motions of a "have to" world as a mother and provider. Barely surviving, but still moving forward, I found myself praying constantly. My prayers came like a fire hydrant from my soul. My faith in God's promise was the only thing I could believe in. Darkness was there, but the light of the Holy Spirit never left me. I threw myself into the things I knew: my job, my church, my single parent family, my chosen family of friends. But, there were so many memories of my past that I was not proud of, and I was still far from okay with myself. I continued volunteering in the Youth and Children's ministry at our church. Then, a Thursday night bible study turned into a full church service where I was able to use my musical gifts in the praise and worship band.

When I began dating again, I found myself in a self-protection mode, which I coined "my Heisman stance" - keeping any suitor at arm's length. Love was an illusion and if it really existed, I certainly thought I did not deserve it. I was convinced that no man on earth could really be out there for me. Who could see past such damaged goods? I prayed for God to send me love, a partner in life. Taking the advice of a sweet older church lady, I wrote down a very specific prayer describing all the traits of the man I hoped existed, my desired gift from God.

Five years after the divorce, I met him. One night, while out singing karaoke with friends, I saw him. He was a handsome man in jeans, boots, white starched shirt, and a chocolate brown felt cowboy hat. He hopped on stage to sing. A week later I saw him again. I tried to keep him at a distance, sporting my Heisman stance, but he wasn't having it. He immediately began attending church with me and attending all my children's sporting and school events. We prayed together every day. He had qualified for the karaoke contest at Wright's BBQ that first night we met, and he was doing very well. After weeks of competition, he had made it into the quarterfinal rounds. I knew the song he was going to sing, "Angel Eyes" by The Jeff Healey Band. The night of the contest, the venue was completely packed with people. The competition was outstanding. When it was his turn to sing, after singing the first few lines, he stepped off the stage onto the dance floor. He sang the chorus, and without missing a beat, he began walking and singing my way. I was sitting in the middle of a very long table surrounded by a group of friends and family. And, with a microphone in hand, during the middle of the competition, he continued singing "Angel Eyes" into *my eyes*. He grabbed my hand and walked me to the dance floor to dance with him while he finished singing the song. That was the night my heart melted. Thanks be to GOD for grandiose gestures of love. We were married in January, exactly one year after meeting. He tells people we met "at the Wright place, at the right time". We are a work in progress, and we still struggle at times in all areas of life. We are both rebuilding, but we are doing it together in Christ.

The August after our marriage we started a part-time business. Our mentor is Lisa Pulliam, a beautiful wife, mother, leader, and friend. When she invited me to attend her second women's retreat, I knew my soul truly needed it. I had never attended a women's retreat. The Christ-centered weekend included worship, praise music, contemplative time, and personal internal exercises that resonated in my heart.

The weekend began with a beautiful, sunny, seven-hour drive to the beach. The next two days it was overcast for most of the day. But, that last day, the day we were to drive home, was as beautiful as the first. So, before heading out, I took one more walk, alone, on the beach.

As I walked along the beach on that last morning of the retreat, the elusive sun finally shone bright and warm. As I walked, I looked down at the shells. There among the full tiny muscle shells were various pieces of broken sand dollars. My mind immediately noted that my human heart desired a full sand dollar. Sand dollars are the beach goer's goldmine after all. People get up early or stay up very late just to search for those whole, beautiful sand dollars. I found myself talking to God, explaining that I did not expect to find a full, intact sand dollar.

As I began my walk back, my mind reflected on all the special moments of the weekend. I thought of our teachings during the retreat, especially our search within for our "I am" statements that came from one of the lessons presented by one of our dear friends Trish Holt. I am beautiful. I am powerful. I am confident. I am a wonderful mother. I am a successful business woman. It shed light on our inner speak - what we really tell ourselves we are. Knowing that our words are so powerful that the more we say, "I am stupid" or "fat "or "scared of public speaking", etc. the more our minds *and actions* make those words true. The hardest part of rebuilding oneself is that negative self-talk: those lies we tell ourselves or have been told by others. People have no idea what it has been like to walk in our shoes.

That was the lesson that sounded in my heart as I walked with my toes in the sand. We are broken just like these shells. We have been broken. We have scars. Some of us are sporting fresh wounds. Some of our wounds are old and scarred and at times have been re-opened, but we came to this retreat. We came, some feeling broken, needing peace, needing quiet, or needing reflection. We do not feel worthy when we have scars, when we are experiencing pain, and when we do not feel whole. Sometimes we feel all alone in our journeys, as if no one else could possibly understand what we have experienced. Therefore, our human instinct is to not pick up the pieces of broken sand dollars...but I did.

I once heard a story about Kintsugi meaning "golden repair". It is a centuries old Japanese art of fixing broken pottery with liquid gold, silver, or platinum lacquer and dusted with powdered gold: revitalizing the piece - giving it new life. The result is that the cracks are highlighted to celebrate its history and its path. The beauty is in the scars.

Staring at the fragmented pieces of sand dollars in the palm of my hand, I saw something beautiful. Like the Japanese pottery, the cracks and the broken pieces of the sand dollars became beautiful to me. I envisioned their beauty as they could be, how they *would be* in the light of the Holy Spirit. God's love makes us whole. It shines through the cracks of our brokenness. Without those cracks, the light cannot shine through.

We are beautiful, we are powerful, we are human...but even more, we are spiritual beings living a human existence. As my walk on the beach came to an end, I thought of the many things in my life that brought me to this point. No one said this life would be easy. It is the hard times, the painful ones that stretch us that make us grow. Those hard times are preparing us for something more. Sometimes that something more is more pain and suffering before our next place of growth. Sometimes we feel smacked and smacked again. Had I not seen those hard times, I would not have been equipped to trust God completely, to follow Him faithfully. I would not have been prepared to help friends in times of loss of parents, of children, or of faith. God grew me up a soldier in His army. Those gold and silver cracks in my armor - that is His love that holds me together and makes me whole. In that moment, the PEACE of GOD overwhelmed me so that I found tears streaming down my face. Not of sadness, pain, or frustration this time, but tears of self-acceptance, of acceptance of this moment, this place in my walk. Thanks be to God for this life, for my children, my grandchildren, my husband, and my friendships. I am not yet where I want to be, but I know that with God's help, I will get to where He wants me to be.

For I reckon that the sufferings of this present time are not worthy to be compared with the glory which shall be revealed in us. (Romans 8:18) Likewise, the Spirit helps us in our weakness. For we do not know what to pray for as we ought, but the Spirit himself intercedes for us with groanings too deep for words. (Romans 8:26-27)

Soul Questions

- We are striving to grow into the most perfect versions of ourselves before presenting ourselves to the Lord. Our personal development is a journey. I have had to find peace in times of hardship. What is a time in your life where you have experienced personal growth through your hardships?

- Though I went through many hard times in my life, I now know that I have had first-hand experience in specific situations that have enabled me to be strong for others. What are some of the scars in your life that have prepared you to help others?

- The definition of **resilience** is the capacity to recover quickly from difficulties; toughness or the ability for something to bounce back into shape. What are some times in your life where you have been resilient?

Please feel free to visit my website www.CourtneyDowdy.SoulsInTheSand.com or to reach out to me via email @ Courtney.SoulsInTheSand@gmail.com My prayers are with you.

Courtney Dowdy

Courtney Dowdy was born in Kerrville, Texas in the heart of the Texas Hill Country.

After graduating Valedictorian of her class in Center Point, Texas, she attended the University of Houston. With the birth of her first child, she shifted from her degree pursuit to begin raising a family. Before settling down in East Texas, she lived in the Texas Hill Country, Corpus Christi, and Houston areas. She has been known by a number of different surnames over the years but plans to keep Dowdy for the rest of her life.

Courtney is an advocate for Breast Cancer and Mental Health awareness. She enjoys fishing, playing the flute, coaching and judging academic speech competitions. She has spent countless hours volunteering in her church in the children's, youth, and music ministries where her passions thrive.

She attributes her personal resilience to being grounded in Christ from birth. Her talents and love of nature stem from her Native American heritage, her parents and grandparents -who were an Assembly of God Minister, a Biology teacher/hunting guide/author, an Emergency room nurse, and a homemaker.

Courtney has spent the majority of her career as an administrative assistant, support staff, and academic coach in the middle division at an East Texas Independent Episcopal School. Serving others and helping others through difficult times brings her joy. Her entrepreneurial spirit keeps her working toward her dreams.

Likewise, the Spirit helps us in our weakness. For we do not know what to pray for as we ought, but the Spirit himself intercedes for us with groanings too deep for words. Romans 8:26

Made in the USA
Middletown, DE
06 December 2018